Virtually Kissing
FROGS

How to Stay Afloat in the Online Dating Pond

by
Julie Willson

LifeEdits

Copyright © 2017 by Julia T. Willson

All rights reserved. No part of this publication may be reproduced, distributed, or transmitted in any form or by any means, including photocopying, recording, or other electronic or mechanical methods, without the prior written permission of the publisher, except in the case of brief quotations embodied in critical reviews and certain other noncommercial uses permitted by copyright law. For permission requests, write to the publisher at the address below.

LifeEdits by Julia, **LifeEditsbyJulia@gmail.com**

ISBN 978-1-944602-11-6 (softcover) | ISBN 978-1-944602-12-3 (epub)

Cover credit: Eled Cernik; interior book design by Janell E. Robisch at Speculations Editing Services (speculationsediting.com); author photo by Dawn V. Gilmore. Graphics courtesy of Janell E. Robisch and Pixabay.com.

Limit of Liability/Disclaimer of Warranty: While the publisher and author have used their best efforts in preparing this book, they make no representations or warranties with respect to the accuracy or completeness of the contents of this book and specifically disclaim any implied warranties of merchantability. No warranty may be created or extended by sales representatives or written sales materials. The advice and strategies contained herein may not be suitable for your situation.

The intent of the author is only to offer information of a general nature to help you in your quest for a satisfactory experience with online dating and to positively influence the world. In the event you use any of the information in this book for yourself, the author and publisher assume no responsibility for your actions. Neither the publisher nor the author shall be liable for any loss of profit or any other commercial damages, including but not limited to special, incidental, consequential, or other damages.

To protect the privacy of certain individuals, the names and identifying details have been changed.

Printed in the United States of America.

CONTENTS

PREFACE iii

INTRODUCTION 1
   Where Can Singles Meet? 3
   Making the Most of Your Online Dating Experience.. 5
   Who Should Read This Book 7
   How the Book Is Organized 8
   What You Will Learn.. 9

THE DATING SITES... 11
   Should You Try Online Dating? 13
   OurTime Site Registration Demo 15
   Let's Talk About...My Site Experiences.....................21
   How to Save Money Dating Online........................ 30
   Pointers from the Pond: The Dating Sites 32

THE PROFILES 33
   Dating Site Profile Features 35
   Profile Summaries..41
   Let's Talk About...Site-Specific Profile Features........ 52
   Let's Talk About...Profile Upgrades 60
   Let's Talk About...Communication Styles 62
   Online Dating FAQs.. 65
   Pointers from the Pond: The Profiles 69

THE SCREENING PROCESS 71
   Basic Screening Criteria 73
   Let's Talk About...My Screening Criteria 74
   OK Cupid Screening: The Questions 81
   Let's Talk About...Screening Potential Mates........... 85
   Unique Requests 87
   How Guys Screen Profiles..91
   Pointers from the Pond: The Screening Process 92

THE SCAMMERS.. 93

VIRTUALLY KISSING FROGS

    How to Identify Scammers..95
    Protection from Creeps and Scammers 99
    Pointers from the Pond: The Scammers 110

THE COMMUNICATION 111
    Effective Dating Site Communication.......................113
    Responding to Incoming Messages 114
    Messaging Potential Matches...................................119
    If You Give a Frog Your Number..............................121
    Messages Received... 122
    Let's Talk About...Sending Onsite Messages........... 126
    Fun with Frogs 136
    Pointers from the Pond: The Communication........ 146

THE DATES 149
    Meeting in Person...151
    Let's Talk About...First Dates 153
    On the Date 158
    My Best and Worst Dates... 163
    Pointers from the Pond: The Dates......................... 170

HAPPY ENDINGS 171

REFERENCES 177

ACKNOWLEDGMENTS 179

ABOUT THE AUTHOR...181

PREFACE

I am writing this book because my online dating experiences have been so horrendous, demotivating, and awful that I want to save others from similar fates. Because in sharing my stories, all my pain and suffering will not have been in vain. Because in the trials that I have endured lie the answers for making online dating a success instead of a catastrophic failure.

Are you sold yet?

I wasn't always this bitter and jaded. Once, just three short years ago, I was a newly divorced woman full of hope and promise. I thought, *Surely there must be hundreds of eligible men who can fulfill my needs and wants.* And now that I was single again, I could explore the possibilities with vigor.

But I'm jumping ahead. Let's back up a little.

Back when I was a single chick in my 30s, there were no dating sites. The primary place people met was in the workplace. In fact, my mother used to casually spread out the newspaper wedding announcements and show me all the happy couples. "Oh, look—most of these people work at [large bank infamous for working their employees so hard they rarely got to leave]. That seems like a GREAT place to meet someone!"

In fact, she was correct. Through a temporary assignment, and despite my degree in psychology from Penn State, I ended up working at a bank (though not that particular one). And after a few years there, I was introduced through mutual friends to

VIRTUALLY KISSING FROGS

a male coworker from a different department, and the rest is history. (Well, now it's the past. Anyway, you get it.)

After two weeks of dating, I knew he was the man I would marry and start a family with. And I did, and we did. And we were happy for most of the next 17 years.

But then we started to grow apart and decided to separate amicably. I relocated to the guest bedroom for a few months until I found a townhouse just eight minutes away. He offered to refinance the house, buy out my share, and remain there with the kids as the primary caregiver.

An atypical arrangement, yes, but one that works extremely well for us. I am more of a tough-love parent, and a little of me goes a long way. So having our preteen kids with their dad for their day-to-day lives—with the larger house, their nice big yard, and their pets (three cats, two leopard geckos, one lop-eared rabbit, and numerous beta fish)—was ideal.

While chatting with a former male coworker during my separation, he mentioned a single guy friend who might be a good match for me.

Wow—this dating thing is gonna be so easy. I already have one on the hook, mere weeks after I decided to divorce!

This would be the first of many experiences that proved one should never get one's hopes up too high.

We met at a local Applebee's. I was a little nervous, but more excited. He was tall, albeit a bit goofy. I tried my best to be charming and witty, although I might have monopolized the conversation a bit because of my discomfort with awkward silences. My date seemed generally annoyed and had nothing nice to say about anything. Making small talk during one of the many uncomfortable pauses, I mentioned that I had start-

PREFACE

ed playing a game on my iPad called Bingo Blingo, to which he responded with an eye roll.

After a few more painful minutes, I decided to call it. Time of death for this date: 1 hour and 15 minutes after it began. After an awkward handshake/hug in the parking lot, he called out angrily, "NO MORE BINGO!"

So maybe this dating thing was not going to be as enjoyable and effortless as I thought. I banished my coworker friend from attempting any further love connections.

Next, I researched local singles groups. There were several listed in my general area, including one for Baby Boomers that met monthly at a local hotel restaurant. This group's members were a bit older than I was seeking, but at least it would get me out of the house to meet new people and practice my social skills.

I attended several events and started to build my confidence slowly. Who knows? Maybe one of these older folks would have younger brothers, cousins, or friends for me! Everyone was pleasant and friendly. On warm spring and summer evenings, we gathered out on the patio to hear live music, enjoy appetizers and drinks, and awkwardly shuffle from table to table for introductions and small talk.

Another singles event was held at a restaurant called Firebirds, famous for their indoor fireplaces that scented the air (and your clothes) with smoke. Only a few people showed up, but I gamely introduced myself to everyone. Shaking hands with one guy, I felt an immediate (maybe even literal) spark.

VIRTUALLY KISSING FROGS

We talked and drank and laughed, barely paying attention to anyone else around us. He admitted that he'd recently ended a six-year relationship and was still in pain, but decided he must get out more. That night was the first time he had done so.

(Spoiler Alert: This, my friends, is what we call a BIG RED FLAG.)

Four hours later, we were the only two remaining of the group. A lingering hug and follow-up texts that evening led to nearly one and a half years of dating. Unfortunately, for much of that time he was emotionally and verbally abusive, and I finally decided that I deserved much better.

After I broke up with him, I spent several months replaying all that had happened and contemplating how to do better in the future. Eventually, I decided that maybe it was time to put myself out there again.

I saw an offer for Match.com on Facebook and clicked to read more about it. Hmm, so I could set up a basic profile, then look through pages of potential mates to decide who might be a great match. Seemed pretty fun and potentially fruitful.

I registered for a three-month trial. Surely that would be plenty of time for me to find a great guy, right? Look how many there are to choose from!

Thus began my adventures in online dating. Once I started getting some interest and responses to my messages, it became quite addictive. I would check the site as soon as I woke up to

PREFACE

see if I had any new Likes or Messages, and examine the new additions in my area.

I started jotting down some of the funny things that happened—amusing profile details, confusing messages, and the like. *Who knows,* I thought. *Maybe someday I'll write a book about life after divorce. This would be an interesting chapter!*

It was a little disappointing that so many guys didn't bother to respond to my friendly messages. If they weren't interested, why couldn't they just send a brief response to let me know? After all, that's what I did. Maybe they weren't active on the site and never saw it. Or perhaps I was coming on too strong. What could I do to make my messages more casual and less stalky?

Aha! How about I offer to interview the guys I was interested in for my book?

So I sent numerous messages reading, "Hey! I was wondering if I could interview you about your online dating experience for a book I'm writing."

I received very few responses, as I recall (maybe none), so I decided to make it simpler and easier for guys to respond quickly without having to think or expend too much effort (heaven forbid).

"If you'd like to schedule an interview, respond with A. If you'd prefer not to be interviewed, respond with B."

This did not pan out as hoped, but it did lead to my very first date from an online connection. One day, a guy replied (using actual words!) and we started messaging back and forth. He seemed nice and attractive enough. We scheduled a call for the interview and ended up talking for over an

VIRTUALLY KISSING FROGS

hour. In fact, we kept communicating by text and phone for several weeks, intending to meet soon for a first date.

By the time that day finally came, there had been quite a build-up of expectations. I figured it had to be better than my first post-divorce experience. ("NO BINGO!")

We met for an early dinner, and were the only people in the restaurant for at least an hour. He was visibly nervous, but the conversation flowed easily and there was a palpable connection between us.

After a few glasses of wine and almost two hours of conversation, I got brave and stood up to sit next to him in the booth.

"I feel like we have a real connection here."

He responded, "Well, we'll see."

Huh? I thought everything was magical and perfect, but clearly he did not feel the same. Seeing the disappointed look on my face, he tried to reassure me. But even though he pulled me in for a sweet kiss in the parking lot, he kept mentioning potential obstacles to us dating (our schedules, the distance), and I ended up in tears driving home. So much for him.

After a brief recovery period, I soldiered on. In addition to Match.com, I registered on eHarmony. Over the next few years, I tried Tinder, Plenty of Fish, and OK Cupid as well. More recently, I've checked out Clover, Zoosk, and Elite Singles. And there are many, many more out there.

Now I know some of you are wondering, "If you're such a failure at this online dating thing, what makes you qualified to give me advice on the topic?"

PREFACE

Well, simply because I have experienced so very much in the past few years. Nearly a dozen sites, hundreds of matches and messages, numerous scammers, and quite a few mortifying dates. It wasn't all bad. Through experimentation and persistence, I have streamlined and simplified the online dating process to minimize pain and heartache for myself, and hopefully for you now as well.

So you can learn from my mistakes and adopt some of my successes. Try the techniques I suggest and see if you have greater success in matching your qualifications and protecting yourself from creeps and weirdos.

And if those don't work for you, go with this: "Those who can't do, teach."

One more thing I should probably mention. I didn't exactly write this book alone. There is a small part of me—unleashed as a result of my years of continual disappointment, resentment, and frustration—who I call Evil Julia. She is always there, lurking in my subconscious, whispering in my ear, sometimes even taking over to send snarky messages or open a can of whoop-ass on a deserving jerk. While I do my best to contain her, she may pop up from time to time. Fair warning, and I apologize in advance.

Now let's get on with it. EJ and I have much to share with you.

What Single People Hate to Hear

For those of you who are coupled up or happily flying solo, please be sensitive to your single buddies. The only thing that's worse than feeling lonely or unloved is hearing one of these things from someone in your life.

- ♥ You're so lucky that you're single!
- ♥ You are so wonderful. Why are you still single?
- ♥ When the time is right, you will find your soul mate.
- ♥ You really need to put yourself out there more.
- ♥ Not everyone is meant to be part of a couple.
- ♥ Maybe you're being too picky/judgmental.
- ♥ You'll find someone when you least expect it.

Feel free to copy this and send it to your friends and family as a not-so-subtle hint!

INTRODUCTION

I like to think I'll just be walking down the street one day and stop and meet someone, like, "Oh my God, you're awesome" and then we start dating.

~ Laura Prepon, actor

Where Can Singles Meet?

There are hundreds of places to find a partner: in the workplace, through mutual friends, at school, grocery stores, gas stations, social gatherings, or the top of the Empire State Building. Wait...I think that was a movie.

At any rate, anywhere there are other people is a potential meet-cute opportunity. And of course we all know that when we stop looking, that's when our true love appears right in front of our eyes. (If I had a nickel for every person who said this to me, I would gouge their eyes out with nickels.) Also, that is tricky if you never stop looking or you rarely interact with people.

According to *Mars & Venus on a Date* (2005), an excellent way to meet your Mr. or Ms. Right is this: "On an airplane, hang out near the restrooms and strike up a conversation while waiting in line. Be sure to walk up and down the aisles to be seen and to see if your soul mate is there." So yeah, there's that.

Then there's the virtual option. For a hard-core introvert who works from home and often hibernates in her little townhouse for days at a time (or for weeks in the winter), where else am I going to meet anyone? There's always the UPS guy who delivers my Amazon Prime packages, I suppose. Although the last time I answered the door in my pajamas and no bra, he seemed to be avoiding eye contact. Sad.

VIRTUALLY KISSING FROGS

There are many advantages to using online dating sites to meet people. What could be easier than sitting comfortably with your phone or tablet, scrolling through a catalog of possible dates, clicking a Like here or swiping right there? You're exposed to hundreds of guys within hours. Where else can you encounter that many people within such a short time period? And you can check in multiple times a day—anytime you need an ego boost. That's another nice perk. You'll get compliments from complete strangers who are awed by your beauty and willing to travel across the world to be with you.

But it's not all kittens and cupcakes, so let me help make the experience productive and pleasant for you.

INTRODUCTION

Making the Most of Your Online Dating Experience

Online dating can seem like a roller-coaster ride. One minute you are giddy and breathless in anticipation about a new prospect…the next, you're plummeting down, confused and discouraged and wondering when the ride is going to end. Here's the thing—as long as you have an active profile, it doesn't end. There will always be guys interested in you who you would never consider dating, and you'll fall in like or lust with hotties who won't give you a second glance.

But by choosing sites that are most likely to meet your specific needs, building an effective profile that showcases who you are and what you're seeking, and communicating clearly and carefully, you will greatly improve your odds of finding an excellent match. He might not be your Prince Charming or one true love, but perhaps a cool new friend, someone to date casually for the summer, or a baby daddy. (Just kidding about that last one—unless that is your objective. Then just be up-front and go for it!)

Sure, there are other books about dating out there. But *Virtually Kissing Frogs* focuses on practical advice and is geared primarily toward women like me—older chicks starting over after divorce, or those who are ready to try something new.

Also, I can guarantee you won't find these examples anywhere else, because they are 100% true stories from my life over the past three years. Even if you never have and never will try online dating, you're sure to be highly entertained by my escapades.

Gentlemen, I'm afraid this book is really not for you. Frankly, the dudes who truly need advice about online dating etiquette probably wouldn't bother reading it anyway. However, for guys seeking tips and advice on creating positive and effective profiles, being respectful in online communication, and enjoying magical first dates, follow me on social media (Facebook and Twitter @vkissingfrogs).

INTRODUCTION

Who Should Read This Book

Any woman* between the ages of 18 and 98, who...

... has dated online and wants to feel she isn't alone.

... is single and curious about trying online dating.

... has avoided it like the Zika virus and wants to validate her decision.

*Disclaimer: The examples and experiences in this book are presented from the perspective of a middle-aged, divorced, heterosexual woman. I cannot presume to imagine what the online dating scene is like for homosexual folks, those still wrestling with their sexual identities, or even hetero men. However, much of this advice can be applied to other types of relationships across the LGBTQIA spectrum (lesbian, gay, bisexual, transsexual, queer, intersex, asexual). And no doubt, the world would be fascinated to hear your stories as well!

What about those of you who are in a great relationship or happily single? Well, my friends, you just keep reminding yourself how lucky you are and laugh heartily at my painful experiences. It's okay, really. I decided a long time ago that I must laugh as well, lest I remain curled up in the fetal position with my face in a pint of chocolate mint chip and surrounded by cats.

How the Book Is Organized

In *Virtually Kissing Frogs*, the topics are organized chronologically, from how to choose the right online dating sites to how to use them successfully to deciding when to take a break, and everything in between.

At the end of each section, I've included Pointers from the Pond for those of you who want to apply the information to your own dating situations.

Throughout the book, you will find personal examples and anecdotes. Of course, to preserve anonymity, no actual names or identifiers are used; however, some have been given froggy nicknames.

While there is no guarantee you will find your soul mate, the information, tips, and advice within this book will certainly improve your odds and give you an advantage over many others. There could be someone out there right now trying to steal your perfect man! You have nothing to lose by trying some of the suggestions here, but so much to gain.

INTRODUCTION

What You Will Learn

Here are some of the benefits you can expect to enjoy from reading this book.

- ♥ Accommodate your desired match qualities and personal situation by selecting the most appropriate dating site(s).
- ♥ Save money by taking advantage of free services offered by some sites.
- ♥ Attract the best potential matches by enhancing your profile.
- ♥ Minimize negative or uncomfortable situations by making more informed decisions.
- ♥ Enhance personal safety through cautious information sharing and communication.
- ♥ Maintain your sanity and positive outlook about dating by knowing when it's time to take a break.
- ♥ Enjoy your online dating experiences more.

Whether you are just scoping out the online dating pond, hovering on the edge of a lily pad ready to dive in, or currently living among the frogs, it's best to make sure you are in the right pond. With that in mind, let's hop over and check out some of your dating site options.

THE DATING SITES

This site is like the clearance section of Walmart.

~ Jersey Frog

Should You Try Online Dating?

By a show of hands, how many of you have NEVER tried online dating but are willing to give it a shot?

Okay, one, two, three...Quite a few of you. Well, good—you've come to the right place.

Now how many have already tried it? Hands up, please.

Wow—so many of you!

And how has it been going so far?

Oh my. He said that before you even met? That sounds frustrating.

He texted you a picture of his WHAT? Oh dear.

Seeking potential mates online is not for everyone. If you socialize regularly or have numerous friends who know you well and have single pals, that's often an excellent way to meet someone. Or if you work in a large office with a variety of people and a steady influx of fresh meat...er, new employees, I mean, you have the opportunity to chat innocently about how to use the copier or what foods to avoid in the cafeteria. This lets you gradually get to know someone to determine whether you have chemistry. As you read earlier, this was how I met my ex-husband.

But not everyone has those opportunities. Maybe you're an introvert who shies away from gatherings and parties, or you're reluctant to trust friends to set you up on blind dates.

VIRTUALLY KISSING FROGS

If you decide to jump in, or want to keep doing it but more effectively and enjoyably, I have plenty of suggestions for you. But you should know that online dating is a whole 'nother animal.

These days, there are dozens—possibly hundreds—of dating sites to choose from. And of course, you are welcome to try several.

I have personally been on nearly a dozen sites. It seems new options pop up every week, many appealing to specific age groups or interests. Some targeted sites include Christian Mingle, SingleParentMeet, and Farmers Dating Site.

OurTime is the largest site for singles age 50 or older. Personal Match, affiliated with OurTime, offers a service where local professional matchmakers will collaborate with you to help you find that special someone. You can easily get started by entering basic information (name, gender preference, date of birth) and creating a username and password. Then you enter some demographics (hair and eye color, height, body type, etc.) and complete a brief profile about yourself and what you are looking for. You can then enhance your profile further by adding pictures, answering questions, and even selecting questions you'd like potential matches to answer.

In fact, I am working through these steps as I write this. Come along and observe as I walk through a typical introductory dating site registration.

THE DATING SITES

OurTime Site Registration Demo

I've already entered the basic profile details noted above and uploaded a few pics.

Looks like the site admins need to approve my photos, so I'll just explore a bit. Today's Matches (presented daily) includes 11 prospects, so I'll go check them out. From each profile, I can view his photos, save the profile as a Favorite, send a message, or send a Flirt, which is a winky face paired with a generic email randomly generated by the site, such as "I like your smile."

Some of the other features I might explore later include:

- ♥ MatchMe (which it won't let me try until my photo is approved) will allow me to discover whether he digs me too before I make a move.
- ♥ ConnectMe (by phone) and VirtualGifts (little photos of flowers or activities) are options I probably won't use.
- ♥ NotifyMe sends alerts for the next seven days whenever he logs in, so I can virtually stalk him (my words, not theirs).

There also seems to be some kind of token system where I suppose you can earn (or more likely buy) tokens, and then redeem them for various services.

Okay, further down I get to the guy's actual profile. He only has one photo—he's wearing sunglasses, and I can't

VIRTUALLY KISSING FROGS

see his teeth. Ooh, that could be an issue. Also, his age indicates 55, but he looks more like 75.

"A little about me" reveals that a sense of humor is important to him and that he "looks for adventures around every corner." That sounds exhausting. "About the one I'm looking for" he neglected to fill out, so I'll just assume he would likely fall madly in love with me at first sight. I quickly become distracted by the "You may also like" options at the bottom, because this dude isn't thrilling me.

Under the Connections section, I can see who Viewed, Fave'd, or Flirted with me, and who Liked my photo(s). Under Who I Like is a summary of My Flirts, Favorites, Views, and Photos that I liked. Over to the right are guys who are currently online and available to chat with. For now, I think I'll select NO for this match.

Yikes, the next one looks like a serial killer. His profile name is DoneWithDramaFun. Huh. So it sounds like he's had some tough times with past relationships and thinks it might be fun to not have drama. He also has a "great sense of humor," according to his minimal profile. But he loses points for spelling and punctuation. That may seem harsh, but as a professional editor, these things are important to me! Another easy nope.

Okay, here we go. Number three has full details on his profile and makes over $100,000 a year. He lives nearby, is toned and athletic…But then I read "I like to smell" within his description, with no further elaboration. This frightens me. Next.

I recognize this next guy from several other sites. I think we might even have chatted once. He has good teeth and loves to read. Whoa! He writes, "If you'd like to email me

THE DATING SITES

with any comments or constructive criticism concerning my profile, I welcome that too." I love a guy who's open to feedback! (And according to my ex, I have plenty to offer.) I decide to send him a message saying that I recognize him from other sites, that his profile is better than most, and that I wish him luck finding his dream girl. I never hear from him again.

Oh, but lookie here! Instead of the site sending my message, it has taken me to a page with various payment plan options, ranging from monthly to six months. The prices are given as weekly amounts, with the actual one-time billing rate in teeny tiny print over to the side. They range from $22 for one month up to their Best Value Plan at $80 for 6 months.

This is a common tactic for dating sites—luring you in with a quick and simple registration and dangling several potential matches in front of your face. Just when you perk up a little…"Gee, this guy seems pretty cool!"…you realize there's no way to contact him unless you pay. And of course, if you are excited about the possibility of a love connection, you're willing to give it a shot, right?

I'll tell you a little secret, though. I've had more luck in terms of connections, messages, and first dates through the free sites—such as Tinder, OK Cupid, and Plenty of Fish—than with any I paid to use. Just sayin'. More on that later.

For now, I'm not planning to invest any money, so let's see what happens if I just click the Continue button at the bottom.

Nope. I thought maybe I could still have limited access without paying anything, but it gives me a billing form instead. Fine. I'll back up and look at a few more profiles. I clicked Yes to a possible match for Guy #3 and the site is

VIRTUALLY KISSING FROGS

encouraging me to send him a message. Nice try, OurTime, but I already know what will happen when I do that. Instead, I click straight over to the next profile.

Option #4 looks grumpy in his one photo and sounds the same with his responses. Do you enjoy going to the movies? "Just OK," he says. Also, he indicates that "fresh breath is important"—multiple times. Makes you wonder what kind of situations he's been in to necessitate that statement, doesn't it?

Oh! A little popup has notified me that someone just viewed my profile. Well, sorry, dude—you probably won't be able to send me a message. Or if you do, I won't see it.

None of the 11 Daily Matches is my dream man, so I go exploring under a different section for new members.

One guy is pretty cute and seems relatively normal. I Like his photo, save him as a Favorite, and send a Flirt. With the Flirt option, the site encourages me to send a message as well. Since I know they aren't going to let me do that, my only option is to return to the search results.

Now I see that I have one message and one Flirt. Dammit! What if it's one of the guys I was interested in? It's probably not. Evil Julia thinks it might be a marketing tactic to entice me to join because they know I just can't handle not knowing. Maybe I SHOULD pay to join—you know, for research purposes. Nah, I think I'll resist for now.

Later that same evening...

Well, here's how they got me: by sending email notifications with enticing but minimal descriptions of the interest-

THE DATING SITES

ed guys who have sent me messages, Flirted, Liked my photos, saved me as a Favorite, etc. While I'm 99% sure those fellas are not ones I would be interested in, the bait they are dangling is just too irresistible. I sign up for just one month for $25. Resistance is futile. I hope you all appreciate the sacrifices I am making for you.

But alas, none of the notifications are responses from guys I liked. Many are from out of state, so either A) they didn't bother to read my profile explicitly stating I only date men within an hour of me, B) they simply don't care and will try to convince me that love conquers all obstacles such as distance, or C) they are fishing blindly and just want a girl to talk to them.

None of these gentlemen had sent messages, but I dutifully send "Thanks But No Thanks" (TBNT) notes, because that's how I roll.

I log off OurTime for now but plan to return tomorrow.

- ♥ OurTime, Day 2: I received one Flirt (not Prince Charming). Whizzed through the 11 Daily Matches presented. Only one possibility, and that was being generous.
- ♥ OurTime, Day 4: Found a normal guy! He's got a great smile, lives close by, seems articulate, and is near my age. I told the site I'm interested and sent him a friendly message...(Update: no response.)
- ♥ OurTime, Day 11: Several days in a row with 11 Daily Duds. And for some reason, there are quite a few (hetero) women mixed in, which I've never

seen on any other sites. I'm chalking this up to the crowded layout and tiny font. Out of courtesy for my grrrls, I sent them all a little note letting them know they need to change their profiles to Women Seeking Men or Women Seeking Women.

OurTime Update

After just three weeks of my four-week membership, I canceled in disgust. In addition to frequent glitches that froze the screen, forcing me to log out and back in repeatedly, the matches overall were subpar and unappealing. Frankly, this site has way too many options and features. With the crowded interface and tiny print, I doubt many older singles find this site enjoyable.

What's that? You'd like to hear about some of my specific experiences on other dating sites? Well, turn the page!

Let's Talk About... My Site Experiences

You can compare various dating sites by searching online. Try, for example, "dating site comparison." Typically, you can find details such as the following:

- ♥ Cost per month (and discounts available)
- ♥ Relationship type (casual dating vs serious folk seeking relationships)
- ♥ User base (total members, male/female ratio)
- ♥ Matching method (from simply age and location to complex formulas based on questions and preferences)
- ♥ Features (chat functions, questionnaires, filters, etc.)

Some of my friends asked me to rate or rank various dating sites based on my own experiences. But that's really tricky to do, because everyone's needs and preferences are different, and of course, each site has pros and cons. So instead, I'll give you my general impressions of the ones I've tried and let you evaluate from there. They are listed in chronological order of when I joined them.

Match.com

My first foray into the online dating world, back in 2015, was eye-opening. Match prides itself on generating the largest number of possibilities compared to other sites. However, I sent dozens of messages and got only about a 10% response rate, which was a bit discouraging. But Match has a decent number of features and has an excellent overall reputation.

eHarmony

Oh, the blissful couples on TV who found their one true loves. I wanted that.

Since eHarmony promotes long-term relationship building, it therefore has quite a lengthy and involved registration process, with hundreds of screening questions to answer and sections to fill out. Theoretically, this laborious process screens out lazy people. After all, anyone willing to spend hours creating a profile must be fairly serious about finding an excellent date, right?

Full disclosure: I did have to tell a little white lie and say I was divorced (though at the time I was still just technically separated), because otherwise I couldn't join.

Unfortunately, despite my specifications to find someone within a 50-mile radius, I was more often presented with men who were way too far away to date—hours and states from me. On the rare occasion I found a decent guy who was close by, there was a complex introduction process unlike any other site I have seen. They refer to it as "guided communication," but Evil Julia feels it implies that we singles aren't competent enough to communicate on our own, instead needing a structured and gradual system akin to arranged marriages. "We'll be the judge of whether you two are made for each other!"

If a guy and I both Liked each other, we then had to answer five questions. Frankly, I don't recall what happened after that, because I never made it much further. I do remember that if you wanted to send an email right off the bat, there had to be written permission from the recipient first. Ultimately, eHarmony's process was a bit too convoluted for my liking, and the matches they presented were mostly too far away.

Tinder

Say what you want about this former hookup venue, but I've had more matches and responses from this free site than any other. Some find it shallow and lazy, since you only need to have a profile name to join. But it is quick and easy. (That's what he said. LOL!) Tinder is also an app, so it's easy to access from your phone or other mobile devices.

The basic premise is to check out the photos and (often minimal) information listed and decide whether you might be interested (swipe right or click the green checkmark) or not (swipe left or click the red X). If the other person likes you as well, Tinder lets you know that it's a match and you can send messages to each other within the app.

You can also SuperLike someone by clicking the star, which lets a guy know you dig him right up front without him having to Like you first. An optional feature called Smart Photos reorders your pics according to the ones that get the most interest.

I spend more time on Tinder than any other dating site because it's fast and I get more matches there than anywhere else. And I met an adorable pilot from Toronto with whom I've enjoyed many delightful evenings when he's in town at a local flight training center.

Plenty of Fish

One of the most robust free online dating sites, Plenty of Fish features a Relationship Chemistry Predictor assessment, which measures five broad personality categories and helps connect you to the best matches. They also have a sister site called MatureQualitySingles for "mature professionals that simply don't have time to waste with other dating services."

On POF (as the cool kids call it), you can browse a seemingly endless list of profiles, send messages, add people as Favorites, and send a Flirt (really just an auto-message reading "Hi there").

If you are not an upgraded member, you cannot view who wants to meet you unless it's mutual. You also cannot view anyone who marked you as a Favorite.

But they do, indeed, have plenty of fish (or frogs) for you to choose from.

OK Cupid (OKC)

This was my favorite dating site overall, partly because it's free (for basic use), and also because it presents thousands of questions you can answer to see how potential matches align with your preferences and values.

OKC calculates match percentages based on these questions, which are grouped into the following categories:

- ♥ Dating
- ♥ Ethics
- ♥ Lifestyle
- ♥ Religion

♥ Sex
♥ Other

They also provide an overall match percentage. I found that having these numbers helped me look past photos that didn't seem enticing at first, and forced me to consider the profile content more carefully. This is how I ended up briefly dating a dude I previously might never have given a second glance—a sci-fi-loving IT nerd who was extremely sweet.

For free, you can send a message and/or click a star to indicate that you like someone. However, only paying members can view Likes, so it's best to send a message if you're interested.

Bumble

One of my local friends suggested I check out this Tinder-like quick-match site. Its unique process puts the responsibility for contact on women: Men can only message women who have shown interest first. In theory, this sounded great for a strong, confident woman like me.

But it seemed that I kept seeing the same guys again and again. And several of them looked like *GQ* models, so I question the validity of certain profiles.

Also, of the dozen or so guys I reached out to, not a single one messaged me back. Well, except for this guy, who responded only after a frustrated note from Evil Julia.

> JULIE: I wish guys would have the balls and respect to reply when someone sends a message.
> FROG: Tell me how you really feel.

So either my matches kinda liked me at first but then changed their minds. Or (more likely) they just swiped on every woman to see who would pick them.

And that was the extent of my Bumbling experience.

Zoosk

New dating sites seem to pop up regularly, and Facebook makes sure to put them right in front of my face because clearly—based on my profile and typical activity—I am a desperate single woman. (Insert exaggerated eye roll here.)

Zoosk uses a behavioral matchmaking technique and was awarded Best Dating Site by iDate Awards in 2016. It also bills itself as "the #1 grossing online dating app in the Apple App Store." Huh. So they're making a lot of money—good for them. After a brief exploration, I can see why.

As with many other sites, they lead you through a simple registration process and tempt you with several profiles. Look how many men are right in my town! Wow—I see someone sent me a message already.

Oh…but I can't view messages unless I pay to join. Oh well, let me take a look at this guy who viewed my profile.

Darn! I can't see that either.

I try being sneaky and revise my profile to include my email address, like a prisoner trying to attach a rescue note to a pigeon from my cell window. "Help! Please come find me if you receive this message!"

Nope. The site must approve all profile updates, and I see the next day that they've added my new content, minus the email address. D'OH!

THE DATING SITES

I guess that's as far as we're getting for now. Sorry, but I'm not made of money, people. I already joined OurTime, remember?

However, their website, The Date Mix, features blog posts about dating advice, online dating, relationships, single life, love and science, and dating data. I found the stats on profile advice—including the best types of photos to upload and keywords that attract more matches—quite fascinating. They also have dating recommendations, advice specifically for those in the armed forces, and other relationship trend data. So go explore here for free even if you don't plan to use their app.

Clover

Yet another up-and-coming app that Facebook suggested I might enjoy is Clover. Facebook clearly doesn't know me as well as it thinks it does.

At first glance, their simple interface appeared somewhat similar to Tinder. Specifically, you swipe right or left based on photos and minimal demographic details, you can only message someone if you're a match, and you can filter by things like age range and distance. Also, both Tinder's and Clover's apps can only be viewed in profile orientation on a tablet, which is kind of a pain in the patootie if my iPad is charging. (Meaning that the plug has to kind of nestle in my belly button. You're welcome for that image.)

Although I could see all the Likes I received (which you cannot in Tinder), in my brief experience with the Clover app, about 90% of the ones I got were from boys in their 20s seeking "cougars." *Hiss, growl.*

A 20 Questions feature allows you to categorize yourself in different A/B options, including whether you are organized/disorganized, are street-smart/book-smart, shake hands or kiss on a first date, or like to experiment in bed. I did not find these especially helpful. Would someone really choose or avoid me because I use a PC instead of a Mac? Also, people can skip questions, or the whole thing entirely.

There is also a feature called On-Demand Dating where you can request dates, even proposing specific times and locations. I tried this with about 10 guys, several of whom had supposedly requested a date with me first, but got zero responses after two weeks. So I am doubtful that these guys were so jazzed about me since they failed to follow up. I wonder if the site is telling random strangers that I want to date *them*. Not cool, Clover.

Another option called Mixers invites you to join various specific groups like Serious Relationships Only (106k members), Make New Friends (13k), 90s Babies, or Fitness Singles. I joined one called Girls That Want Nice Guys and asked, "How does this work with 30,000 people on a group chat?" Apparently, it doesn't. No one responded or even acknowledged my presence.

I hopped back on to the site after being away for several weeks and was presented with most of the same guys I already vetted. It was a frustrating waste of time and made me wonder if they are still fine-tuning their process.

EliteSingles

Okay, Facebook. This is the LAST ONE I'm trying, for real. Good thing I wasn't too busy with editing work the day I discovered this site, because I spent over an hour

THE DATING SITES

completing an extremely detailed inventory of characteristics about myself. *Wow*, I thought. *They must have some complex matching algorithms. Maybe this is finally a site that will provide quality options!*

That sure was time-consuming, but I'm finally done—PHEW. Wait...what? Now I am on a page with various payment options. Oh, I see. It's gonna be like that, huh?

Evil Julia 😈 and I are too exhausted to go any further.

So as you can see, each site has benefits and limitations. Most dating platforms allow at least a small peek into their sample offerings for free, but every one of them charges for access to all their features and functionality.

I got the best results from Tinder, OK Cupid, and Plenty of Fish while using their free options. The biggest waste of money was a full-year subscription to eHarmony. I only purchased it because it seemed like a bargain at the time. Plus, I figured I could use it for book research even if I didn't get great matches. Truth be told, I didn't invest much time there because most guys were so far away, and as a result, I found not a single match. SUGH (sigh + ugh).

Speaking of investments, next you'll get some advice about how to date online most cost-effectively.

How to Save Money Dating Online

It may seem that dating sites only exist to make a profit and don't even care if you find your soul mate. Well, duh—that's pretty much true with any business. However, there are a number of ways you can save money and still seek your honey bunny.

Compare rates and membership options across sites. Because they tend to evolve and change frequently, I suggest you research current pricing and reviews when you're ready to dive in.

Check for special introductory offers. Dating sites have more competition than ever before, and this can work to your advantage when they dangle lower rates as bait to lure you in.

Try out any free offerings. This will give you a taste of what to expect in terms of features that are important and the types of guys who are there. You might decide that the complimentary features are all you need. Or if you want to invest in a membership, you'll be able to make a more informed decision about the one(s) that fit you best.

Consider a lengthier membership. While a one-month payment of $30 may seem more reasonable than paying for 3–6 months, you might be better off paying a higher amount overall if it works out to a lower monthly rate.

THE DATING SITES

Oh, you're planning to find your dream guy within just a few weeks and won't need to be on that long? That's great. Then you won't need to worry as much about the money spent. Alas, I'm afraid the more likely scenario is that you'll have to kiss many, many frogs to find a good one, which takes time and patience. Or perhaps you'll date briefly, decide he's not "the one," and jump back in.

Share with a single pal. Get together with a friend or two and review profiles together. If you like someone, either hop on to the site yourself and search for him, or have the member send a message on your behalf. Then you can communicate by text or email. While I've never tried this, one of my friends did entertain herself for several hours selecting fellas she thought might be great matches for me (and laughing hysterically at my limited options).

A final cautionary note about dating site memberships: Be careful to check the fine print when you join any site as a paying member. Some of them automatically renew behind the scenes without any notification.

Pointers from the Pond: The Dating Sites

- Research online dating sites to see which one(s) might suit you best.
- Consider trying several at a time.
- Explore sites thoroughly once you join to familiarize yourself with features.
- Save money by using free features or special offers.
- Partner with friends to explore multiple platforms at once.

Once you've hopped in to the right pond, how do you make your lily pad appealing so that all the best frogs will leap over each other to get to you? Read on, my friends.

THE PROFILES

I believe that behind every man is a strong woman. I'm currently incarcerated in federal prison looking forward to my release date. I just need that special someone in my life.

~ Felony Frog

Dating Site Profile Features

Most online dating profiles include essentially the same basic information, but each site has its own unique fields and features. Let's start with the basics, then I'll tell you about the outliers.

Basic features on most dating site profiles include:

- ♥ Photos
- ♥ Profile name
- ♥ Demographics about the person
- ♥ Summaries (who they are, what they are seeking)

A Picture is Worth a Thousand Dates (Or at Least One)

Most profile templates require at least one photo, although they don't seem to care if it's a picture of you or your dog, your truck, or the American flag instead. You can sometimes upload up to a dozen, but this varies by site and level of membership. Some are quite serious about it and insist that each photo be "approved" before it is displayed, even encouraging other members to report anyone who violates their guidelines—for example, with nudity or profanity. And yes, perhaps Evil Julia has reported a few.

While perusing men's profiles, I often wonder: *Is that really the best picture you could find to lure in your dream girl?*

VIRTUALLY KISSING FROGS

What decade is that from? And why are there so few people who have figured out they should angle their phones from the side for mirror shots instead of holding them directly in front of their faces?

Interestingly enough, I came across an article in *The Dating Handbook for Dudes** with must-have photo ideas for their online dating profiles. This explains a lot.

- ♥ You MUST have at least one pic of you holding a fish. This applies to all sites, but is critical on Plenty of Fish to show that you appreciate the metaphor.
- ♥ What woman doesn't enjoy a sexy pic of a dirty truck or motorcycle? Just don't drive away with her heart, you stud!
- ♥ Lounge in bed and strike your sexiest pose. Advanced technique: Channel Blue Steel's pouty fishy face.
- ♥ Mirror and car selfies tell your suitors, "I don't have any friends who can take my picture, so think about how much time I'll have for you!"
- ♥ A group photo with multiple guys gives her a fun challenge! "I wonder which one is him? I hope it's not THAT one."
- ♥ Have at least one pic aligned sideways for variety. Consider adding a note: "This is what I'll look like next to you in bed. Kisses!"
- ♥ Include a shot that is blurry and out of focus to showcase your mysterious side.
- ♥ If you love your pet, don't be afraid to include him in every picture. Let her know how dedicated you can be to a living creature. Formal portrait from JC Penney with your Chihuahua? Priceless.

THE PROFILES

- ♥ Ladies obviously need to see what you look like naked or shirtless. If you display a full body tattoo of an eagle across your back or flex in front of gym equipment, all the better!
- ♥ BONUS POINTS: Include only one picture on your profile, but not of yourself. Try one of these options: Baltimore Raven (the mascot, not a football player), a brown bear, a beach sunset, or a large pile of money.

*I hope you realize these are sarcastic suggestions that guys should avoid for best results, not an actual book (that I know of). But yes, they are all real examples I have seen in the wild.

Then again, you shouldn't make too many assumptions based only on photos. A message was sent to me from a guy with a do-rag, wife-beater tank top, and a torso full of tattoos. I thought, *Oh goodness—what's this guy got to say?*

But his only comment was "I love your dress." And when I replied, "Thank you," he simply responded "yw" (you're welcome). Well, that was nice.

Profile Names

Each site requires you to choose a profile or username when you register. Some people use a variation of their actual name, while others get much more creative. Here are several I've encountered that I found amusing.

- ♥ CougarHunter
- ♥ Donut_Taster (He was a cop.)
- ♥ Lets_Do_It

- ♥ Mooncrow
- ♥ sandboxcatpoop
- ♥ MINDMENTALIST (What other kind of mentalist is there?)
- ♥ SaltyNuts
- ♥ PassionThorn
- ♥ darkbeige
- ♥ LOONERANGER

Headlines

Some sites also include a headline, which allows for up to about 30 characters to express who you are or what you're seeking. These can also be quite entertaining.

I think this is a good time to mention that I have left some of the misspellings in examples for entertainment's sake. These are in **bold text** so you know my editor, reviewers, and I left them there intentionally.

- ♥ no
- ♥ nice black
- ♥ No big women
- ♥ **Awaiting** for that special somebody (Evil Julia🌹 says he might be "awaiting" a while.)
- ♥ I feel this is a waste of time
- ♥ Looking for a soul-sucking psychopath

I suggest keeping your tone positive here. (You catch more flies with honey, right? And we know how frogs love flies!) Aim for short and sweet, keeping in mind that your headline might be the only thing he reads.

THE PROFILES

Demographics

Demographic details typically include information (in no particular order) about the person themselves, in addition to their match preferences. Most are optional.

I've listed these fields alphabetically. This section can include any of the following:

- Age
- Ambition level
- Astrological sign
- Body type
- Car (As in, do you have one?)
- Children (There's usually a number here.)
- City
- Do you do drugs? (Some have an option for "Only soft stuff, like marijuana.")
- Do you drink? (For example: never, socially, like a fish)
- Do you want children? (I assume they mean MORE children, and not the ones you already have.)
- Education (For example: finished high school, some college, college, advanced degree)
- Ethnicity
- Eye color
- First name (Optional, but handy when it's not part of their profile name)
- Gender (Usually this is obvious...but not always.)
- Hair color

- ♥ Height (In feet and inches, sometimes also listed in centimeters)
- ♥ Income range
- ♥ Intent/Seeking (For example: friendship, casual dating, serious relationship, marriage)
- ♥ Occupation/Profession
- ♥ Personality (category, not whether you have one)
- ♥ Pets (The usual cats, dogs, birds, bunnies...but also reptiles, insects/spiders, and other)
- ♥ Religion
- ♥ Smoking (For example: never, social, regular)
- ♥ Status (For example: never married, single, separated, married, divorced, widowed)
- ♥ Where I grew up

Interests

Some sites, like Plenty of Fish, include space for various interests, which are typed in freeform, making for some interesting results.

- ♥ Woman
- ♥ Motorcycles Boats Cars Women Tractors
- ♥ I like fiction books because they are not real
- ♥ I am passionate about education and helping people who **wants** to be helped
- ♥ No games no rushing no crying no complaining
- ♥ I am 175cm tall and I weigh 80kg. My favorite drink is red wine and my favorite food is potato with sauce and fried chicken.

Profile Summaries

How much detail should you include in the written portions of your profile? At least enough to let guys know who you are and what you're seeking. Be honest and specific. If you're looking for a serious relationship, make sure to say that outright. (Although there's no guarantee anyone will actually read it. About 90% of my Likes were from men who never viewed my profile and only saw the primary photo.)

Most guys' profiles on sites like OKC and POF have just enough information to go on. Some are quite lengthy (even several pages long), with amazingly detailed descriptions of exactly what they expect from a woman in their lives. Like this dude.

> I find a voluptuous body type to be the finest physical expression extant of feminine beauty. Three elements beyond this harness my attention: alabaster skin, practically untouched by the sun; wide hips, accentuating the temple nucleus of female energy in near proximity; and butterfly wings, that most luxuriant of features to mark the adult divine.

I've also seen many profiles like this:

> JUST ASK

Certain phrases pop up frequently, as you can imagine. If I had a dollar for every time I saw these, I'd be rich...and would probably run away to live on a private island by myself!

- ♥ I'm an easygoing/laid-back guy
- ♥ No drama
- ♥ I will fill this part out later
- ♥ I don't like talking about myself, but here goes
- ♥ I love anything outdoors
- ♥ Not looking for a pen pal
- ♥ Looking for my partner in crime
- ♥ I like all kinds of music...except rap
- ♥ I'm not looking for someone who's perfect, just perfect for me
- ♥ If we meet offline and you look nothing like your pics, you're buying me drinks until you do

Some fellas are open and honest about who they are and where they are in life at the moment...

- ♥ My moral values are my own, and higher than most of **societies**
- ♥ I am gorgeous that's why I don't have my picture up cause I only want to attend to pretty ladies like you
- ♥ I do have tattoos but only 6
- ♥ I'm younger than the wind but older than my teeth
- ♥ I been **divorce** 3 times so at least you know now... and yes I have tattoos on my head and no I don't use steroids...and yes I live at home with my parents...I ain't **Rick** but I ain't poor either

THE PROFILES

...up-front about their finer qualities...

- ♥ I can be a little on the **Macgiver** side that I can fix anything and can rescue us from situations
- ♥ I have great teeth, sleeves on my shirts, and smart enough to have a quality conversation
- ♥ I have 4 pet rats that I adopted from a rescue...they are fun and a bit more wild than the rats I have had in the past

...or candid about what they want.

- ♥ Please make sure you're in my league
- ♥ I want hot babe can be my wifey to keep. I love to have baby boy with my girl if she can
- ♥ Please let your weight be in proportion to your height
- ♥ In search of a woman that really wants to get to know me, not just want to smash
- ♥ I find cleanliness and a pot belly on a woman sexy
- ♥ I would like to live the rest of my life with some one that love me and I love her and we would do great things for the lord (**A men**)
- ♥ I have a very low mileage penis and I intend to keep it free of warts, bumps, and pissing fire or making more babies
- ♥ I wish I was an octopus so I would have 8 hands to touch your butt with
- ♥ I don't wanna get married, I just want someone to pack me a lunch, cook me dinner, and rub my back every night. If you can do this, I'll get you a stupid ring and let you prance around in a little white dress in front of your friends and family for 1 day!

And yes, sometimes what they want is a specific sexual situation, a la *50 Shades*.

- ♥ I have an interest in "romantic restraint"—restraining a partner with scarves, ropes, or other—but also respecting their wishes.
- ♥ Married with kids and looking for something casual, yet ongoing. Someone submissive. Not looking to change my situation or yours. Not an open marriage.
- ♥ Daddy looking for his baby girl for a loving Dominant/submissive relationship. I have a loving yet firm hand. Don't be shy.
- ♥ You will be an absolute equal by day, but happily offer complete surrender by night. At the end of the day, after brushing teeth and washing up, you will put restraints on your own wrists and ankles before coming to bed. This signifies that, until we arise to face the new day, you are handing yourself over to me completely.

This guy below (as I recall, he was an actor) clearly has his ideal woman all figured out. Do you think he's being realistic?

Turn-Ons: I really love a confident, attractive, smart, fit, funny, alluring, accomplished, interesting and refined woman who has a career and interests of her own and is somewhat well traveled and savvy, with an appreciation for the arts and music, theater, opera, ballet, and symphony, but also classical rock, blues, and jazz. Simply put, she's smart, but sexy and feminine, too. She should also be someone I can trust. Fi-

THE PROFILES

nally, I absolutely adore an affectionate woman who can take the lead in romance and intimacy.

(I hardly expect to find the girl of my dreams who satisfies all my wants and needs, but like everybody else, I hope to come pretty close. I set my standards pretty high.)

Others use their profiles to showcase their sense of humor:

- ♥ Headline: Here I am…your next big mistake
- ♥ I have style, but I must admit I buy what the mannequins are wearing
- ♥ Lost a lot of brain cells doing drugs in college. I may occasionally stare at you and drool. Don't worry, it passes. Also, I may still be doing drugs now. I can't remember.
- ♥ Tried bringing sexy back and all they'd give me was store credit
- ♥ Perpetually horny massive smartass who hates people and picks his nose (and lists his job as Chief Masturbator, Self-Employed)
- ♥ Remember that messages with naked photos get special consideration
- ♥ How do you get Dick from Richard? Just ask!
- ♥ When I have the time, I look at naked pictures of tribal women in old copies of *National Geographic*
- ♥ I'd like to meet someone who reminds me of my mother
- ♥ The beard is not a symbol of my appreciation for co-op markets or artisanal beers. I just don't like shaving.

- ♥ If you're very short, I may unthinkingly try to rest my drink on your head. It's best to wear high heels or sit on a stool.
- ♥ My ex-girlfriend lives with me. She's booby-trapped parts of the apartment. Haven't used my own bathroom in months.
- ♥ First date suggestions: strip club, hot dog eating contest, Bronx Zoo (monkeys only), staring contest, butter sculpture show
- ♥ Hobbies: talking shit about people behind their backs, objectifying women, feeling sorry for myself, making plans I will never follow up on, solo hide-and-seek (aka hiding practice), writing down lies I told so I can remember them later
- ♥ I have one roommate. Her name is Friday. She's my cat and she's adorably precious and tiny. I hold the distinction of being voted best roommate by her six years running which I'll also point out is how long she's been alive.
- ♥ I would love to meet someone in the healthcare field as my therapy bills are getting expensive. A girlfriend/therapist combo would be awesome!
- ♥ Need new dating technique. Daughters are too old to take for walks in the park and plus the leashes made the girls uncomfortable.

Then there are those who emphasize what they absolutely do NOT want.

- ♥ I don't do clubs, so if that is your twist, keep it pushing.
- ♥ I hate cell phones and people obsessed with selfies or Facebook.

THE PROFILES

- ♥ Love the Lord and I don't do drama.
- ♥ Please make sure you're in my league. I'm not Brad, but it seems some of you fancy yourself as Angelina. You're not.
- ♥ I don't love your dog. No one loves your dog but you.
- ♥ If you used the phrases "partner in crime" or "I love to laugh" or "I've got my shit together" we're probably not meant for each other.
- ♥ You should message me if: **You** not older, fatter, or uglier than me.
- ♥ PLEASE stop bragging about how you can get sex anytime and **your** not on here looking for sex. Cause if you meet a guy you like on here, don't tell me you **would've** give him a piece of the cookie if **your** digging him.

Clearly, some dudes have had awful experiences in the past and are now proceeding with extreme caution.

- ♥ Headline: I quit
- ♥ About Me: I'm done I'm done I'm done
- ♥ Please don't pester me with 20 questions and waste my time unless you're ready, willing, and able to meet
- ♥ No more baggage, no more tolerance in the name of love, no selfish cheating woman
- ♥ The past is dead and I like to keep it that way
- ♥ I don't like liars, drama queens, or tramps

And boy would I love to hear some of the stories from these next guys!

- ♥ I'm done with niceties, here's the brass tacks. Quite frankly, I don't have the time to waste on the wrong person. AGAIN.
- ♥ I don't fall for overly horny, pervy chicks cruising the internet looking for innocent men to take advantage of.
- ♥ When I give you my home number, it does not give you a license to stalk in the middle of the night, EVERY night...because it'll make me think you're really a MAN, since most really needy guys always do that.
- ♥ If you think you'll have thoughts of grabbing the scissors and letting them loose on my little head when I'm asleep after our first fight? Let me just say, the mental hospital is not the same thing as my home address!
- ♥ I don't have **neither** the time **nor** the desire* to drive to PA, DE, NJ, VA, or even DC.** Please do not contact me if your profile contains:
  - A bathroom pic
  - You are making fishy-lipped duck faces
  - Wearing more makeup than a clown
  - Older than me
  - Contains the words diva, fashionista, princess, or foodie. Just added—sapiophile. Give me a break!

* ♥ Nor a grasp of double negatives.

**Fun activity: Find a map and guess which state he lives in! (PA = Pennsylvania, DE = Delaware, NJ = New Jersey, VA = Virginia, DC = Washington, DC)

THE PROFILES

Remember the actor? Unsurprisingly, he had plenty to say about what his ideal woman should NOT be.

> Turn-Offs: At the top of this list is betrayal of trust...too painful to deal with again. I'm not into lowbrow broads with tats and piercings, leather and chains, heavy drinkers with too much baggage, heavy smokers, overweight slugs with no interests, no education and no class. Just don't want any drama in my life. Can't stand unnecessarily argumentative, always contrarian, overly jealous, excessively controlling, stifling, suffocating, constantly needy, annoyingly whiny, dependent women with no interests or career of her own.

Hope that's not too harsh.

Many profiles have disappointed me on an editorial level. (Sassy comments contributed by Evil Julia.)

- ♥ My personal life is really high maintenance because I like good **stuffs** and I can say looking good is my **hobbies** (Guess spelling is not one of his "hobbies.")
- ♥ You have **too** live life **too it fullness**. Please **say focus** on the prize.
- ♥ i need a **girlfiend**
- ♥ Interests: **exedra** (I assume he meant "etc." or maybe Excedrin for a headache?)
- ♥ It takes two to tangle (Technically correct, but likely not what he meant.)
- ♥ Last Book Read: **Angles** & Demons
- ♥ Last Book Read: Webster's **Dictonary** (Guess he didn't get to the Ds yet.)

VIRTUALLY KISSING FROGS

- ♥ I am seeking **your** wife who is faithful caring loving who loves cooking cleaning taking care of **his** man (Pronouns are hard.)
- ♥ I am very funny, outgoing, **intelligence,** and honest (Are you, though?)
- ♥ **Anyting** I own I try to make it **uneak.** I like to be **differant** but not **outragus.** I am **curiuse** about the paranormal. (I can't even.)

...and others that left me scratching my head.

- ♥ I am an easy man who **make** life easy
- ♥ Looking for a good
- ♥ I don't care for ugly looking food
- ♥ Look young for comfort, tranquility and slave partner who makes me feel the warmth and tenderness and stability (Wut?)
- ♥ Very Ambitious (Yet he completed About Me and First Date sections with "..." so I doubt it.)
- ♥ He likes "fine **dinning**" and "had a glass of coke with a slice of lemon in it while i was in **rome** that i just can't seem to forget." (Ah yes, Italy is famous for its delicious soft drinks.)
- ♥ I love to chat and talk on the phone. (This was repeated about 30 times to fill up the screen. Yikes.)

I swear the profile entry below is real. Setting the blatant sexism aside, what exactly do you think this guy was smoking?

> LOOKING FOR MY TREASURE. ARE YOU ON HERE? need to, would like to kayak more (have two, we can paint one pink for you!) also need to

bike more, am sure there is a yard sale somewhere we can pick you up a strawberry short-cake bike… Looooovvvvaaaa the beach, a blanky, chair, reading material, cold beverage, good eats…HALLLAAA!! COMMUNICATION IS THE KEY, OMG!!!!!

Let's Talk About...
Site-Specific Profile Features

OK Cupid Profiles

The OKC app displays profiles with essentially the same details as other sites—photos, age, city/state. (I find city/state more helpful than current distance because, of course, people move around.). Also, there are spaces for other details they choose to share, such as height, whether they have children, languages they speak, whether they drink or smoke, etc.

Then there's a self-summary. I must admit, these are much more robust than you might expect, especially compared to Tinder.

Other sections within the profile include:

- ♥ What I'm doing with my life...
- ♥ I'm really good at...
- ♥ The first things people usually notice about me...
- ♥ Favorite books, movies, shows, music, and food...
- ♥ Six things I could never do without...
- ♥ I spend a lot of time thinking about...
- ♥ On a typical Friday night I am...
- ♥ The most private thing I'm willing to admit...
- ♥ You should message me if...

Below that are questions, listed by the categories with highest matching percentages. And yes, you can dive right in to see exactly how they responded to questions that you also

THE PROFILES

answered. (If they answered some you haven't yet, you can answer then and immediately see results.) This is often quite entertaining, as you can imagine.

At the bottom of the profiles are a few descriptors with up or down arrows. The one I'm looking at right now shows ↑ Sex-driven, ↓ Conservative, and ↓ Wholesome. So no mystery what he's looking for, is there?

Following are some amusing profile details I have seen on OK Cupid:

- ♥ Entire Self-Summary: helpful (Note: This summary was not helpful.)
  - Occupation: Employee
  - I study, play volleyball **2–3wk** (How much does that pay, I wonder?)
  - Scholar (But indicates he likes to "**socialisze**" and is most grateful for "**everyuthing**.")

- ♥ I'm really good at...
  - Good in my work aspect, Baking **muffin**, reaching high places
  - Being incognito / You should message me if: 59 6f 75 20 73 65 65 6b (I wonder if anyone broke his code?)
  - WebMD-based medical self-diagnosis

- ♥ Six things I could never do without...
  - I'd have to say steak is high on the list, my neck pillow, I use my inversion table most days, I always carry my pocketknife, a lighter & chapstick

VIRTUALLY KISSING FROGS

- Duct tape, my friends, can't think of 4 other things

♥ What I'm doing with my life...
- **Taken** care of sin and family
- Well I'm on here so can't be much

♥ I am passionate about...
- Education and helping people who **wants** to be helped

♥ Favorite part of a woman...
- **Bussum** and **Botox** (Guessing he meant bosom and buttocks?)

♥ First Thing People Notice...
- I don't know what it is, but there is definitely something different about me. (He looked like Carrot Top. Google as needed.)

♥ The most influential person in your life...
- I would like to handle everything by myself due to I have been like this for a few years

♥ The most private thing I'm willing to admit...
- Even though I can be a whore, I never sleep with multiple women at the same time. I'm afraid I'll get 2 women pregnant. LOL

♥ Favorite books, movies, food...
- Food: Yes please (This was a sturdy fella.)

♥ Interests: Fun / About Me: have fun / First Date: whatever

- Interests: **ect** / About me: **ect**??? (I don't think he knows what et cetera means. Or how to spell it. Or abbreviate it.)

Plenty of Fish Profiles

Profile demographics are fairly standard, but this site has a few unique questions. One is "How ambitious are you?" I prefer someone who is Very Ambitious; the other extreme is Not Ambitious, which I imagine is him lounging in sweatpants covered in Cheeto dust and playing Xbox.

In the Personality category, you can select from labels such as Athletic, Beach Bum, Blue Collar, Class Clown, Geek, Hopeless Romantic, Player, and Princess. I classified myself as a Bookworm because there was no option to write in Sex Goddess. (Evil Julia is rolling her eyes.)

Also, if a person has completed the Chemistry Test, you can click to review their results in a variety of areas such as:

- Easygoingness (Pretty sure they made up this word.)
- Family Orientation
- Openness
- Self-Confidence
- Self-Control
- And an overall summary: How does your personality affect your love life?

What you're reading in the Chemistry Test section are general comments based on responses given, not their actual verbatim answers. For example, "Based on your responses, you are low in self-control." Then there is a generic description of how this typically manifests itself in relationships. These may be useful for those who value such particular traits in a partner.

I rarely looked at any of these, but I did give virtual bonus points to the guys who took the time to complete this introspective exercise. It's a good indicator of how serious they are about finding the right woman, don't you think?

Profile categories include:

- ♥ About Me
- ♥ Conversation Starters (formerly labeled First Date)
- ♥ Extended Profile (This is an option only for upgraded users, and frankly, I don't recall what is in there.)

POF features a section called Will Respond, displaying users who are most likely to respond based on their site history. Also, Top Prospects shows your best relationship prospects, but usually this is just whoever most recently sent or responded to a message, so I'm not sure how predictive it truly is.

You can view potential matches that are closest to you under the Nearby tab. They also have an Events tab that displays local happenings. But the ones I can view at the moment are anywhere from New Jersey (doable) to Staten Island, New York, and Stamford, Connecticut (not so much).

Under My Matches, you can peruse a large page of people quickly by looking at only one photo for each, along with username, age, and location. For those who seem promising, you can click to view their full profile. A page called Ultra Match ranks your options by compatibility (according

THE PROFILES

to what, exactly, I don't know). You can also refine these by age, distance, or when they were last online.

Under Meet Me, you can swipe or click Tinder-style (but also access their profile for a deeper look). Also, here is the They Said Yes tab, which currently shows 264 fine gentlemen who want to meet me. Alas, I cannot view them unless they send me a message, which is the only time I would want to meet them anyway! Finally, It's Mutual displays matches I liked who liked me back.

The Viewed Me tab comes in handy to see dudes who have looked at my profile.

Ah yes, I see you viewed me last night, MrCuddleBear. So this means you saw the message I sent and you went back to look at my profile again. But then you decided to ignore me. Then WHY DID YOU SAVE ME AS A FAVORITE in the first place?

Sorry about that! All of Evil Julia's feelings are flooding back now that we're on these sites again. Let's move on, shall we?

Tinder Profiles

Profiles on Tinder are some of the briefest ones you'll ever see. They can literally consist of just a name (or code name) with no photo, age, distance, or description. However, most include at least those few details and a photo or two.

If you log in via Facebook (which I imagine most people do, because it only takes two seconds), Tinder will show you Common Connections—1st are people you are friends with, 2nd are friends of friends, etc. This can also influence your decision. For example, if they are buds with a bunch of rowdy alcoholics. Or with your ex-husband.

For those of you who are curious, here is my current Tinder profile.

> Julie, 49
>
> (Employer) Edits by Julia
>
> (School) Penn State University
>
> Seeking someone sweet, funny, and affectionate for casual dating (but not just sex)
>
> **MUST LIVE WITHIN 30 MILES OF MIDDLETOWN, DELAWARE!
>
> You should be 5'9" or taller, with a nice smile.

Despite the brevity of this profile, of course many guys still ask me what my name is and where I live. And you'd better believe they lose points for doing so!

Here's one of the lengthier profiles I've seen on Tinder. You can tell he has thought this through, and I admire his honesty.

> Sometimes I just don't know why I date. Would I rather hook up? Yep
>
> Will we go out to dinner? Probably
>
> If we exchange numbers, will I send you dirty pics? Probably
>
> Do you have to like kids? Nope…and you probably won't meet mine

THE PROFILES

Do I travel more than an hour for a date? Ehhh, maybe

Would I expect a kiss and maybe more? Hell yes

Do I do more than kiss on the first date? Yep

Call him uncouth, but least you know what you're in for.

So that's the scoop on profiles from the sites I've used. Read on for some tips about when to update your online details.

Let's Talk About... Profile Upgrades

If you have been active on a site for several months, or are rejoining after a break, make sure your information is current.

Other reasons you might want to consider updating your bio include the following:

- ♥ To add something new about yourself, like a new hairdo or significant weight loss.
- ♥ To upload more recent or additional photos that are flattering and showcase your personality.
- ♥ To try different approach—for example, by streamlining your content. One format I like is About Me/About You/About Us, with bullet points for each.

Also, make sure you include details that showcase you as an awesome partner and minimize anything that comes across as bitchy, picky, or high-maintenance.

Take a look at your existing information and consider these questions:

- ♥ Does this accurately represent how my friends would describe me?
- ♥ Do I sound confident but not cocky?
- ♥ Are my expectations realistic?
- ♥ Would I respond to a profile like this?

THE PROFILES

Finally, avoid any specific dates or seasonal mentions unless you plan to revise frequently, as these become outdated quickly. For example, you probably don't want viewers seeing "Happy Holidays" when it's June.

Some sites offer a professional revision service to upgrade your existing profile, presumably with the intent to improve your odds. I paid $35 to try this on Match, but felt their version was wordy and way more than most guys would bother reading, so I never used it. However, I've tweaked and upgraded my profiles repeatedly over the years to keep them fresh and current, and I suggest you do the same.

In my experience, it seems that photos are much more of a factor for dudes than written comments, which—let's be honest—many times are skipped altogether. Especially when you post a bathing suit shot showcasing your assets. And yes, I did try this as a little experiment and I did see an upswing in Likes, Favorites, and Messages. But will that attract the type of guy I'm truly looking for? Not so much. I'd much rather have him like me for my wit and charm and flawless punctuation.

And speaking of punctuation, let's take a moment to discuss the importance of communication in terms of profile content.

Let's Talk About... Communication Styles

As a Learning & Development Specialist (fancy name for a trainer) at a global bank, I facilitated a fascinating workshop based on a perceptual style theory, which is described essentially as six distinct lenses through which people view the world. This shapes our preferences and tendencies, and influences our behaviors.

About a third of people in the world prefer a direct, to-the-point style of communication. In fact, if your message doesn't capture their attention within the first few sentences (or in some cases, the subject line or header), they may stop reading entirely. In terms of dating profiles, this could explain why many people simply look at photos and a few key pieces of information to decide whether you're right for them.

Another third prefers some background information before making a decision. So on dating sites, you might explain why someone should choose you, or how their life may be more wonderful with you in it. To appeal to these folks, you could also include stories or vivid examples to showcase your personality.

The rest of us require comprehensive details to feel confident, or at least an opportunity to ask for additional information. So in terms of dating profiles, this would equate to completing every field, answering every question, and providing a thorough summary of yourself and your pref-

THE PROFILES

erences. And perhaps an invitation to message you with any other questions they might have.

What does this mean for profiles that include minimal information? That's right—about 66% of us will breeze right past those or swipe left because we simply don't have enough to go on. I mean, unless you're a stone-cold hottie.

Or if your profile is too lengthy and detailed, some people who might have been interested could get turned off, thinking, "Oh geez, they have a whole encyclopedia here. Who has time to read all this? She seems pretty high-maintenance. Ain't nobody got time for that!"

In addition, within the past 10 years or so, we've grown more accustomed to communicating in fragments—think text messages, memes, or subheadings within blog posts—and are much less likely to bother reading long passages of content.

So because all different kinds of people will be viewing you, try to appeal to each of these communication preferences when you are drafting or revising your own profile.

Put the big stuff right up front, in simple terms—in the headline, if possible. One of the headlines I've used is "Sweet and Sassy Seeks Funny and Snuggly."

Use bullet points instead of lengthy paragraphs. (Tip: You can use arrows [>], or if you want to get fancy, create a bulleted list in MS Word, then copy and paste it into your profile.)

Consider designing it as a sort of commercial for yourself with examples about how awesome you are.

Include enough detail that someone with a need for extensive information will feel confident they can make an informed decision.

Do NOT assume anyone will read your profile from start to finish. (Although as a detail person, I almost always do!)

Think about the type of man you want to attract, and make sure your profile is designed to maximize the chance of that. If you want an intelligent guy, make sure your summaries are articulate and grammatically correct. If a sense of humor is important in a mate, express your playful side in your responses.

Online Dating FAQs

So…you've joined a dating site, completed your profile, and have started viewing potential matches. Now what?

Here are some best practices to make the most of your time and money.

How long should I plan to actively use a dating site?

No one can predict the future, but based on my experiences, it's best to allow several months to find someone worth dating. If you choose to pay for membership, cost will be a factor in this decision as well.

I would caution you against a year-long membership. Odds are that you will find a number of good guys to date well before then, and if you don't, you might want to take a little break anyway. Optimism and hope are critical qualities for this adventure!

Trying a site for three months gives you time to assess whether it fits your needs and provides the type of matches you're seeking. If you love it, you can always extend your membership. Or you might want to check out a different site to see how it compares.

Should I try out multiple sites at once, or just one at a time?

The more hooks you throw in the water, the more fish you are likely to catch, right? So if you're eager to mingle, experiment with as many as you want. For example, you could join one paid site such as Match.com while exploring some free ones like Tinder or OK Cupid as well.

Consider using different photos on each, as an experiment to see which ones get the most attention. (And remember, Tinder's Smart Photos feature can do this for you automatically.)

Then again, as you will see later in the book, the whole process can become overwhelming in a hurry, and you don't want it to take over your life. If you're just interested in testing the waters a bit, one at a time might be enough.

Do you see the same people on different sites?

Sure do! And they saw me as well, as I was often on multiple dating apps. Of course, each one has slightly different details, so this allowed me to learn a bit more about them. But if I Favorited or messaged them previously with no response, I didn't bother stalking them on a second site.

Well, maybe once or twice…to see if I could trick them into liking me so I could say, "AHA! How come you like me now but you didn't on the other site? Because my hair is longer? Oh, it's the swimsuit pic where my boobs are hanging out, isn't it?"

Evil Julia😈, come on. I didn't really do that. Much.

How often should I check for matches?

This depends on how motivated (notice I resisted saying "desperate") you are to find someone and how much free time you have. At first, the curiosity of wondering who is out there, and the little thrill when someone shows interest, are quite addictive. I spent many nights early on scrolling and clicking for HOURS before I realized that the room had gone dark and I'd forgotten to eat dinner.

If you have other things to do in your life—like sleep and a job and whatnot, which you definitely should have—I suggest you pace yourself and let technology help out where possible.

You can enable notifications on your mobile devices to alert you when someone has checked out your profile, matched with you, Liked you, sent a message, etc.

My preference was to jump in maybe once or twice a day to see who viewed my profile so I could view theirs as well. Also, I used that time to look through any new matches being offered.

Why does it seem like all the best guys ignore me?

Many theories exist about this. First of all, you know from all the clichés your friends and family spout at you that there are "so many fish in the sea" and "you have to kiss a lot of frogs before you find your prince." While in real life, you might encounter two to three singles in any given day, the online scene has thousands. This is great in theory, because we have so many to choose from. But it perpetuates the idea that even if you find someone decent and cool, there are likely other fish and frogs that are better—sexier, funnier, richer.

So although at one time we might have contented ourselves with a person who was kind and sweet and good enough, now we tend to be less satisfied. We have higher expectations and standards that are sometimes nearly impossible to meet.

With this in mind, consider relaxing your expectations a bit. Maybe pick three top deal-breaker qualities instead of a top 20, which rules out anyone besides Chris Pratt or Jennifer Lawrence. (I'm guessing they are not currently on any of the dating sites anyway.)

Consider chatting with someone who doesn't fit your typical ideal—someone with wildly different interests. You might be pleasantly surprised!

Pointers from the Pond: The Profiles

- Take the time to complete online dating profiles thoroughly. If you indicate "Will complete this section later," make sure you actually do so.
- Upload several high-quality photos, with at least one full body shot. If any are older than a few years, mention this as a caption or within your summary so it doesn't appear that you are trying to be deceitful.
- Be honest and specific about who you are and what you are seeking in a mate.
- Think about your ideal match and tailor your information accordingly.
- Consider different communication preferences when drafting your summary. Detailing your entire life story or listing everything you hate will turn many people off immediately, and leaving most fields blank will give potential suitors very little to go on.
- Update your profile with more current photos or information every few weeks or months to keep it fresh.

Once you're in the pond, you'll need a method for deciding which frogs are worth your attention and which are too slimy to bother with. Read on for advice about how to assess each frog carefully.

THE SCREENING PROCESS

I did the online dating thing...There was this one guy who, when I asked him what he did for a living, said he "used to be in a band."

I was like "That is not an occupation."

~ Julie Klausner, comedian

Basic Screening Criteria

As you've learned, sometimes you have very little to go on when perusing profiles. I use the following chart as a guide to sort through them quickly.

	SURE!	PROBABLY NOT	HELL NO
PHOTOS	Appear recent, nice smile	Teeth issues; pics fuzzy or sideways, or mostly of dogs, truck, motorcycle	His expression says, "I'd really love to tie you to a tree."
PROXIMITY	Within 30 miles	One-hour drive	3,000+ miles
HEIGHT (I am 5'8")	6' or taller	5'8" or shorter	"Doesn't matter when we're horizontal."
ACTIVITY LEVEL	Snuggler: Netflix and chill, as the kids say	Active: hiking mountains, running, biking	Every pic a reflection from gym mirror with muscles flexed

Let's Talk About...
My Screening Criteria

I consider a number of factors when reviewing online dating profiles, some more important than others.

Distance

I live in northern Delaware, in a small but bustling place called Middletown. We have all the major fast food restaurants, two movie theaters, a bowling alley, mini-golf, and tons of shops and restaurants. Yes, it's a tiny state, but I like it. We are conveniently located near many fun and fabulous destinations, such as the beaches of Rehoboth and Dewey, Baltimore's lovely Inner Harbor, the rolling hills of Pennsylvania Dutch country, funky Philadelphia, and even New York City.

I typically request matches within 30–50 miles of my location, depending on the available options. As noted, some sites are better than others at staying within these parameters. (I'm looking at you, eHarmony!) And Tinder uses your current location, so if someone's traveling, they can check out locals who might be down to meet for dinner, show them around town, or have wild monkey sex.

I am surprised at how many people ignore location and distance entirely. I've received messages from the West Coast, and even from other countries, with many men indicating that distance is no obstacle to true love. For more than a year, I dated a guy who was nearly an hour away. It

THE SCREENING PROCESS

was doable, but not ideal. So consider how far you are willing to travel for a romantic connection.

Photos

Assuming the guy lives reasonably close to me, I next check out his photos.

He should appear clean and well-groomed. His teeth must be decent. They don't have to be perfect or bleached white, just not crooked or rotting (eww). In at least one photo, he should be smiling instead of looking miserable or psychotic.

Let me clarify—he should be smiling in at least one photo and not look miserable or psychotic in ANY of them!

I will likely pass if I see any of these:

- ♥ Sleeveless shirt in a restaurant (armpit hair and food are not a good combo)
- ♥ Tribal tattoos or tats of Jesus or a cross (most others are acceptable, even sexy)
- ♥ A shot looking up from below, showing multiple chins and a menacing glare
- ♥ More pics of his dog(s) than himself (cat photos are allowed in unlimited quantities)
- ♥ He's holding a gun or a dead animal he has just killed
- ♥ He is giving the finger
- ♥ Sideways pics (if you can't even figure out how to orient a photo, I'm afraid we're not an intellectual match)

Height

Guests must be at least 5'9" to ride. (No, I do not actually have this wording on any of my profiles. One can only imagine the responses it would encourage. *Shudder.*) But here's the thing: I'm 5'8½" in flats, so any dude shorter than 5'9" is just not going to be attractive to me.

I tried! I briefly dated one who was 5'7", but every time we walked side by side, I felt like his mother. And when I went to put my arm around him...well, it just felt silly.

If a guy's height isn't provided, it's one of the first questions I ask. Of course, this requirement is listed in my profile as well, but as you know by now, many don't bother to read that and many others simply disregard it, perhaps assuming they will win me over with their charm and wit. Like this guy:

> **JULIE:** How tall are you?
> **FROG:** I'm 5'4"
> **JULIE:** Hmm. I'm 5'8", so that could be an issue.
> **FROG:** How about if I say I'm 6 feet?

Aww, bless his heart. But still a no.

Age

As of the summer of 2017, I was 49. (And that's gonna be my permanent age from now on, FYI.) I typically search for men between the ages of 38 and 58ish. One thing that really surprised me is the quantity of young guys in their 20s on these sites who lie about their ages in order to present themselves to "cougars" in their 40s and 50s. I suppose they are seeking more experienced lovers. Or perhaps

THE SCREENING PROCESS

women who no longer have to worry about birth control? But make no mistake, in my experience, they are generally hyped-up horndogs with no interest in anything real or meaningful. So beware!

Here's one of my young paramours, age 22:

> We talked awhile ago. Asked to be you're boytoy. Let me know if you changed you're mind.

Can you guess my response?

If your answer includes the word "NO" and something about spelling "your" correctly, you're a winner!

Another potential suitor sent this enticing message.

> Any interest in a well-endowed boy toy? Kinda being thrown out there by roommate, says I need an older that knows how to work a big c***.

I assume he just forgot to include the word "woman" and didn't mean to call me "an older." However, out of curiosity (you know, for research), I attempted to get to know him a little better. He admitted, "Just so you know, I'm not going to be an ass, but not gonna treat you like a princess either."

Ladies, here's a tip: If the guy only talks about himself and what HE wants, run fast and far.

Then again, older gentlemen are often set in their ways and less flexible about accommodating new people in their lives. Sadly, some of them seem to be seeking an ideal woman who is less likely to exist the older they get and the more rigid their standards and expectations become. That's certainly not to say that you can't find true love and partnership later in life. My aunt fell madly in love at the age of 55, so by that timetable, I still hold out hope.

Consider casting a wide net age-wise—you can always toss back any that are too young or elderly for your liking.

Profile

First of all, the profile must be completed. Quite a few have only placeholders such as "..." or "I'll fill this out later" or "??"

If a guy can't be bothered to take a few minutes to reflect on who he is and why he is even on the site, it's unlikely I will give him a second look, no matter how gorgeous he may be. In fact, a hot guy with an empty profile often makes him seem like more of a douchebag. It's as if he's thinking, "I'm perfect and amazing. No time for stupid words—I'll just wait for the ladies to fall at my feet."

I also consider the overall tone. Is he just talking about himself and what he likes or hates? Does he sound bitter or jaded about the whole dating process? I'm much more likely to Like or message a dude who seems positive and hopeful about finding a cool chick and is generally content with his life.

Political Leanings

Without getting into sides here, let's just say I have extremely strong opinions about this topic and have little respect for those who skew to the other side. (In fact, on Tinder I've added a note that guys who support the "other" side can just go ahead and swipe themselves.)

If this is important to you, look for indications about whether he is conservative, liberal, or middle of the road. OK Cupid

Writing Ability

Yes, as a lover of words—reader, writer, editor—the ability for my suitor to form coherent thoughts is a turn-on. Did he take time to form complete sentences and use basic punctuation, or did he just bang out random words and text abbreviations from his phone. LOL? TBNT.

I'm not talking Shakespearean prose here...just sentences, or even neat fragments, with most words identifiable as standard English. Otherwise, I reflexively cringe, shake my head, and move on quickly.

Here are some examples that made my eyes bleed (figuratively, of course) and no doubt made my editor twitch.

- ♥ Hello **lady's** I'm looking.
- ♥ What I'm not is a night in shining armor...i,m way out of my **elimate** trying to convince someone that I'm the man of **there** dreams. Looking for someone I can share my day with and listen to **there's.**
- ♥ Not into the Bar **seen.**
- ♥ Anyone can say anything about **themselfs** on here.
- ♥ I spend a lot of time thinking about...Thinking **alots** different **think.**

I HAD to send feedback on this next one—the irony was just too strong.

- ♥ By the way, if your profile looks like **you're** text messages (lots of misspellings), please keep moving.

Here are some other reasons I might swipe left or move on:

- ♥ If he looks like an ax murderer, or someone who might keep body parts in his basement.
- ♥ His comments are in broken English. (Sorry, words are super important to me. Also, certain accents are a huge turn-off, though I haven't found a way to express that without sounding racist.)
- ♥ Look, here's one with four photos: a sexy Hispanic schoolgirl, a police car, some colored scribbles, and a sunset. What the hell am I supposed to do with that?
- ♥ It's clear by his shirtless pose, pouting bed selfies, or comments ("Want to hang out?") that he's just looking for sex or friends with benefits (FWB).

As I mentioned earlier, some sites feature additional screening options. OK Cupid was one of my favorites.

OK Cupid Screening: The Questions

OK Cupid presents hundreds of questions and calculates match percentages by category, which I find especially helpful for determining whether a fella aligns with my wants and preferences. However, you should be aware that a percentage may be low simply because they only answered five questions, and sometimes it's low for no apparent reason at all.

After looking at the overall match percentage (ideally 75% or higher), I turn to the category with the lowest percentage match, where I often find deal-breakers that knock them out of contention, such as a YES to any of these questions:

- ♥ Do you sleep with the television on?
- ♥ Have you ever spent more than 8 hours playing video games?
- ♥ Do you have an ex that you would really like to date again?
- ♥ Do you think drug use with your partner can be a romantic activity?
- ♥ Do you ever use the word "slut" to refer to a woman?
- ♥ Would you consider dating someone who has vocalized a strong negative bias toward a certain race of people?

- Would you for any reason read your mate's email or pose as them online without their permission?
- As an adult, have you ever worn a leash and dog collar in public?
- Would you ever film a sexual encounter without your partner knowing?

Or these responses…

- Do you enjoy intellectual debates on topics like politics, religion, science, or philosophy? YES, I LOVE TO ARGUE
- Are you a cat person or a dog person? NEITHER
- How often are you open with your feelings? RARELY
- About how long do you want your next relationship to last? ONE NIGHT
- How frequently do you bathe or shower? ONCE A WEEK OR LESS
- Which best describes how often you get WICKED DRUNK? OFTEN
- What is your preferred cuddling position? DON'T TOUCH ME
- How often do you brush your teeth? RARELY / NEVER
- Do you litter? OFTEN
- Do you pick up after yourself? NO, I LIVE IN FILTH
- Which of the following do you consider to be the best explanation for the existence of human life on Earth? HUMANS WERE BROUGHT TO EARTH FROM THE STARS
- Which is bigger—the earth or the sun? EARTH

THE SCREENING PROCESS

- ♥ If you lived with your partner, how much time would you spend naked while in your home? ALL OF THE TIME
- ♥ "Your a bitch." What bothers you most about this sentence? The profanity / The grammar / NEITHER ONE BOTHERS ME
- ♥ How does the idea of being slapped hard in the face during sex make you feel? AROUSED (I said HORRIFIED.)

How would you answer this one?

Imagine that you come home to find a partner pouring red wine all over a stranger's naked body and then licking it off. Which, if any of the following, would bother you most?

- A. The spilled wine
- B. The cheating
- C. The fact that I was not invited to join in
- D. This would not bother me

This whole question bothers me, including the poorly worded phrasing. (It HAS to be "one of the following" or you can't answer the question.)

And this one is just wrong on so many levels. Note the variety of comments that accompany this response.

Do you think homosexuality is a sin? All of these said YES.

- ♥ Technically yes, but I'd watch two girls kiss all day.
- ♥ But like all men, I see nothing wrong with two **woman** together.

VIRTUALLY KISSING FROGS

> ♥ I believe with everything God gave, he gave choice. I believe that we are all capable of murder, and it is your choice to sin or not sin. But like all men, I see nothing wrong with two women together—double standard, yes. Sorry, I'm a man. (Note: This man also indicated he would be willing to pay for good sex. Is that not a sin? Hmm.)

This one really makes me wonder about the people who work at OK Cupid and come up with these questions.

Do you feel there are any circumstances in which a person is obligated to have sex with you?

But then you see a response like this and it all makes sense. (Not really.)

> No. Well, actually the answer can be yes if it's an unusual case. Say for example that hostile extraterrestrials are holding the entire planet hostage and will completely destroy the Earth if a woman doesn't have sex with me. Under those circumstances, the woman in question is probably morally obligated—it would be her duty to the entire planet, wouldn't it?

Let's dive deeper into the best ways to use all this information to your advantage when deciding which frogs to pursue.

Let's Talk About... Screening Potential Mates

Why is it important to screen matches carefully?

If you love going on dates or having nice meals with strangers, then maybe you're not as concerned about vetting someone thoroughly before you meet. For an introvert such as myself, I only want to meet a dude in person if I already feel some sort of connection and have run him through all the filters I can beforehand. While it may be a longer investment of time to text for a few days, it protects me from the agony of a lousy first date.

If he prefers camping in a bug-infested tent to lounging by a resort pool, or doesn't laugh his ass off watching *Deadpool*, no amount of chemistry will overcome those factors for me. Maybe for you it's finding a guy who shares your passion for travel or your love for reptiles.

Is it possible to be too picky?

Certainly, and you've seen some ridiculously finicky examples already. If you've got a vision of your ideal mate that is so specific it includes eye color, head shape, and beauty marks, perhaps you might consider relaxing your requirements a smidge. That being said, you should absolutely stand firm on your deal-breakers, and never settle for less than what you truly want and deserve. You may not have

VIRTUALLY KISSING FROGS

fireworks and strong chemistry initially, but you want to at least feel a comfortable connection.

You tend to come across certain situations repeatedly on dating sites. Continue on to see a few common categories from male profiles.

Unique Requests

The Adulterers

- ♥ I'm married, but we have an understanding.
- ♥ Profile indicates "Separated," but that turns out to mean that his wife has banished him to live in the basement with the dog.

I came across a profile with one photo (body shot with head not visible)—a cop who openly admitted in the summary that he was married and cheating. Curious to learn more about why and how someone would do this, I chatted with him online for a bit. He had two young kids, and his wife had no idea he was on the site. He told me they did have sex, but it was too "vanilla" for his liking.

> **JULIE:** You don't feel guilty?
> **FROG:** Sure, I struggle with that, but I have needs.

According to his profile, he is Christian and believes it's a sin to be homosexual. But apparently adultery is okay.

The Bi Guys

- ♥ I am a bi-curious submissive male seeking a dominant female for FLR (female-led relationship).

I had quite a lengthy and fascinating chat with this gentleman. He referred to me as "Ms." and seemed sweet and sincere. I must admit, as thrilling as it sounded to have a guy

VIRTUALLY KISSING FROGS

live only to please me and do absolutely anything I wanted (which I never quite achieved with my ex-husband—LOL), I thought it might get annoying after a while. Also, I wasn't too keen about attending the support groups he mentioned, nor about the possibility of leading him around town with a dog collar and leash.

Then there was the bisexual guy who seemed more excited about confessing his homosexual experiences as a teen than about getting to know me. He claimed I was "the only person he'd ever admitted this to," but I doubt that. I felt like I should have billed him for a psychotherapy session.

The Danny Downers

- ♥ I punch in and out of work **everyday** and usually just **lay** around afterward
- ♥ After many years of wasted time, I lost many of my life's passions including traveling the world…

The Female Fanatics

- ♥ I have three rules of life. 1) All men are scum. 2) There are NO exceptions to rule #1. 3) Any of the aforementioned who use mental or physical intimidation are beneath even the dignity of pond scum. Women are a superior, more evolved creature. I am a pro-woman man. They should be worshipped.
- ♥ I should be doing the cooking and giving the backrubs. My place is to serve. What the lady wants, she gets. Simple philosophy.
- ♥ I am quite willing to make sacrifices and compromises to accommodate the needs of my fair damsel.

THE SCREENING PROCESS

In theory, this all sounds great. But you've gotta wonder what compels them to make such bold statements.

The Fetishists

- ♥ Looking for women **whom** "give" golden showers
- ♥ Friendly and attractive couple seeking playmate
- ♥ I have certain interests that would probably repulse 40% of the mainstream, cause internal reflection of 45%, and intrigue maybe 15%.

One guy informed me that he preferred to wear women's undies. In fact, he had quite the extensive collection, with hundreds of options. He started texting me daily for my recommendations on fabric, color, and style. Once he sent a full photo shoot of him cleaning his apartment in a French maid outfit. I had no issue with his apparel choices, but I realized quickly that he was much more into himself than he likely ever would be with me.

The Guy Helpers

- ♥ I don't know how to say this but my Boss was really intrigued by your profile. He's 56, white Caucasian...

This dude spent a lengthy paragraph trying to convince me that his boss (a high-ranking player in DC) was a great catch and that I should give him a shot. He provided an email address so I could contact the man directly, and I was sooo tempted to use it just out of curiosity. But then I remembered all those movies where a person is standing innocently on the sidewalk when a black van screeches up, then someone jumps out and throws a bag over their head and tosses them inside. So instead I politely declined.

How Guys Screen Profiles

> A young and undiscerning man can even feel physical chemistry by looking at a naked store mannequin.
>
> ~ *Mars & Venus on a Date*

From my perspective, guys typically screen for...well, boobs. Next question?

I'm joking of course, but the majority of Likes and messages I receive are from guys who haven't even viewed my profile. Sometimes, Evil Julia quizzes them: "Specifically what makes you think we'd be a good match?" At which point they either give up or begrudgingly go scan it and randomly pick out one or two things. "Umm, I like to watch movies and eat food too."

My best advice here is to use current photos and try to summarize key points in the headline or at the top of your profile. And you can always ask right up front, "Have you read my profile?" as a not-so-subtle request to do so.

Pointers from the Pond: The Screening Process

- Try to look past a guy's photos initially and read the profile. Maybe he's your dream guy but just doesn't photograph well. EJ🐸 says you can always put a bag over his head.
- Identify your deal-breaker qualities, but try not to have too many. Train your eyeballs to locate those details first to speed up the screening process.
- Take advantage of the supplementary information, such as OK Cupid's question bank, to further sift through your matches.
- Be open to getting to know men outside your usual preferences. Consider widening your net in terms of distance or age. You just might be pleasantly surprised.
- If you're on the fence, just go for it! Sometimes you simply have to take a chance. At best, you'll meet a cool person and have an interesting chat. If he's not so great, at least you'll get a good story out of it. At the very worst, he could be a creep or a stalker, but you're in luck—we're covering that next!

Not all the frogs you encounter are cute and innocent. When you're in the online dating pond, you must know how to weed out the bottom-feeders and remain safe and secure on your own lily pad.

THE SCAMMERS

Hello, sweetie. You have a great smiles and I would love to know how you feel about men in uniforms.

~ Faux Frog

How to Identify Scammers

Honestly, when I get a message from someone with broken English who claims to be in the military, I feel…like he is probably a scammer.

One thing I never expected to deal with when I first tried online dating was wading through such a large number of fake profiles. Not only does this decrease the number of truly eligible matches, it's also frustrating and infuriating.

Why do people set up fake profiles on dating sites?

For people who legitimately want to find a mate, there are a number of reasons they may lie or embellish the truth. Perhaps they don't feel confident that someone will be interested in them as they truly are—for example, in terms of appearance if they don't think they are attractive or tall enough.

Sadly, some of these people are trying to play a long con where they attempt to get you to fall for them—or at least pity them—so you'll send money. The most extreme example of this technique, where a person poses as someone else entirely, is called *catfishing*.

What are some warning signs that might indicate someone is a scammer?

- ♥ Photos appear to be fake (such as from a magazine) or don't match the description
- ♥ Tells you they are new to the site
- ♥ Claims to be widowed (sometimes also raising one child)
- ♥ Gives multiple names, all of which sound very "American"
- ♥ Communicates in broken English but claims to be native to the United States
- ♥ Says they are in the U.S. military, but are currently overseas or just about to deploy
- ♥ Tries to get you off the site immediately ("Here's my number, I prefer to chat offline.")

Classic Scammer Profile

I've learned to recognize certain features that are common to most scammer profiles. Honestly, it's as if they're all using the same *Scamming for Dummies* guidebook. Conveniently, the post below showcases many of them in one location. The letters explaining red flags are described below.

I am single for 3 years now, my fiancé died in an auto crash **(A)**, I have been in the US army **(B)** for 19 years...presently am on deployment to Nigeria **(C)** but my Facebook brought my location to tinder **(D)** and I am retiring in the next 3 months **(E)**, I am looking for the woman I call my

THE SCAMMERS

own, that is the reason I am on here and I just joined on here **(F)** but I have not been an active member **(G)**.

- A. Widower status to elicit empathy
- B. Member of armed services to show commitment to America
- C. In a dangerous, remote location so they will conveniently be unable to talk over the phone or send photos
- D. Attempt to explain why Tinder shows he is within 30 miles when he claims to be thousands of miles away in Africa
- E. Upcoming promise of retirement to keep you hopeful that you'll get to meet soon
- F. Claims to be new to the site, which makes him seem vulnerable and naïve
- G. Excuse for not visiting the site more frequently

Here is another example. See how many red flags you can identify!

> **FROG:** I'm new to this dating site. I have been a **widowed** for 6 years now, I have a 11 yrs old son, I'm a Military Investigator and stationed in Afghanistan for peace keeping, I'll be back in 2 months time for retirement. Any problem with me?

Odd that he asked that last question, but I went with it.

My reply:

> **JULIE:** That story seems very familiar. Yes, I do have a problem with you because I'm pretty sure you're a scammer.

VIRTUALLY KISSING FROGS

There was no response.

Once you've identified someone as a potential scammer, then what? Read on to hear how you can keep yourself safe from these predators.

Protection from Creeps and Scammers

How can I protect myself from creeps and scammers?

Be vigilant for the warning signs I mentioned. Could a man be a true widower and not a scammer? Absolutely! But if you see several of these in combination, tread carefully.

If you get a phone number, do a reverse lookup (whitepages.com). Results will indicate whether the number has been associated with previous scams or fraud. Also, check the area code to see what state it's from and whether that makes sense based on what he's told you.

Be cautious when sharing information. I'm sure your mother warned you many times about giving out personal details to strangers. Once you've gotten to know someone over a period of weeks or months, use discretion and share more as you feel comfortable. But until you've actually met in person and perhaps done some online research, stay in self-preservation mode.

Heed your gut instincts. Does something seem "off" about him? Does he seem to have an agenda or be following a script instead of communicating naturally? Is he ignoring your questions and comments?

Ask as many questions as you need or want to. If he refuses to answer, that could be a clue that he is following

Scamming for Dummies. Then again, he might just have poor communication skills or simply be a selfish a-hole. But in any of those cases, why would you want to keep talking to him?

If the dude is making you uncomfortable, take action immediately. Every dating site has an option for blocking members who are behaving inappropriately. Look into this as soon as you join a site, so you know exactly how to block someone quickly to avoid further contact. If the guy has your phone number, block the number so you will no longer receive calls or texts.

Then take a deep breath, celebrate the fact that you protected yourself from a jerk, and let karma handle the rest.

I once found a real cutie, and we flirted back and forth for several days. Feeling ready to meet in person, I asked for his last name (he already knew mine).

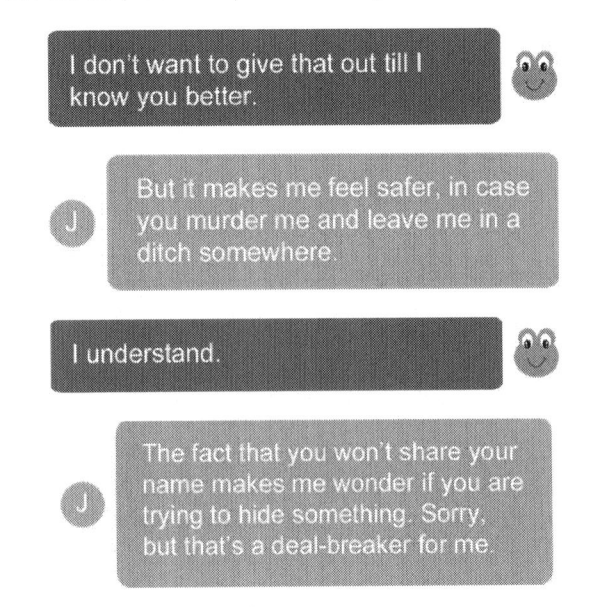

> I don't want to give that out till I know you better.

> But it makes me feel safer, in case you murder me and leave me in a ditch somewhere.

> I understand.

> The fact that you won't share your name makes me wonder if you are trying to hide something. Sorry, but that's a deal-breaker for me.

THE SCAMMERS

> I'm not trying to hide anything, I just want to be discreet. I had a bad experience before.

Turns out that a former FWB was kind of stalking him, accessing his ex-wife's Facebook page and driving past his house. Yikes. So it's great that he was protecting himself. But ladies, we have to be just as cautious! With all these warning bells going off, I decided it was best to hop away from this one.

How can I protect others from creeps and scammers?

If you feel someone is behaving inappropriately (sending lewd messages, using profanity, displaying nude photos), block first, then use the Report feature. Many sites ask for a specific reason you are reporting the person and provide several options, such as "Inappropriate messages or photos" or "Possible spam."

Some members include in their profiles a message such as "If you are a scammer, swipe left." Nice try, but if someone truly thinks they can scam you out of money, I doubt they will heed such a warning.

Here are some additional encounters where I was able to protect myself by doing a little research or using site features.

Busted!

JULIE: So when did you live in New Hampshire?
FROG: I never live in New Hampshire.

JULIE: Yes, I figured. But your phone lived there— that's a NH area code. (Confirmed via White Pages reverse lookup.)

Fun With Maps

FROG: I'm currently in San Antonio.

JULIE: That's odd, because Tinder shows you are currently 28 miles away from me.

FROG: I'm new here don't know much about this.

JULIE: New in the country? Well, then you should know that Texas is more than 28 miles away from Delaware.

Name Game

JULIE: So you said your name is Eric on Tinder, but your email has Mark in it, and you signed the name Andrew. Which one is it?

FROG: Eric is my name, I am a Catholic and Andrew is Baptism name. My dad's name is Mark. So I just use Andrew Mark at first to know each other.

THE SCAMMERS

So Many "Language"

J: Hmm, Tinder indicates you are 16 miles away from me.

Yes babe. Cause that where I live back in state, am on deployment now in Libya will be back in state very soon.

J: I don't think that's how Tinder works. It's supposed to show your current location. So you're not American. What is your nationality?

LOL Am an American of cause. Don't you no the meaning of getting deployed Am a military man

J: Yes I do. But I am a writer and editor and can tell when someone is speaking non-native English.

LOL Ohhh yeah you correct. Cause I have an accent...I study so many Language cause of my field in the military. So what why...I can speak 5 good different language correctly. It's like you kidding me...or using me to catch fun.

Other Fishy Frogs

- ♥ I'll love to make friends with you to see where this would **leads** to cause starting with friends would make things **more** stronger and efficient
- ♥ Am sorry it's really dangerous to send messages through phones in a foreign base like mine, might give off signals to terrorists
- ♥ Actually **I'm** live at Columbia in north Carolina but on work right now in the western region of Africa now, hope this doesn't end our chat too soon?
- ♥ Am Joe from United **State**

Caught But Clueless

FROG: Good morning dear how was your night? I hope you had a good night's rest and your morning is going well i am working now and a little busy but thought i should say hey and i hope to hear back from you soon we can get talking on phone later today if you don't mind have a lovely day email me or leave your email i want for us to share pictures if you don't mind. Talk soon

Aha! Now I had his phone number. I did a reverse phone search and his number had a note indicating that it had been associated with "asking for money." So I called him out about it. His response:

> **FROG:** I must say i really don't understand you. i am not asking for help i am proud of my achievements

The next day, he pretended as if I had never brought it up.

> **FROG:** Good day dear, how has your day been? Have not heard from you i hope you slept well and i hope your day is going well…email me when you can i have been very busy but will make out time for us to talk on phone i look forward to talking to you dear.

And later…

> **FROG:** Hey sweet one i can call you in a few minutes when i will finish and get ready for bed,,,my day has been super crazy busy, you are on my mind and i really want to catch up with you on phone and also plan our meeting soon so our chemistry can trigger and we can make plans on working out a relationship as we both know that this is what we both came on the match site for…i hope you understand me dear…you are always in my thoughts

Needless to say, he didn't call.

Tinder Bad Day

This is one of my favorite online conversations ever, and just the perfect ending to a crappy day.

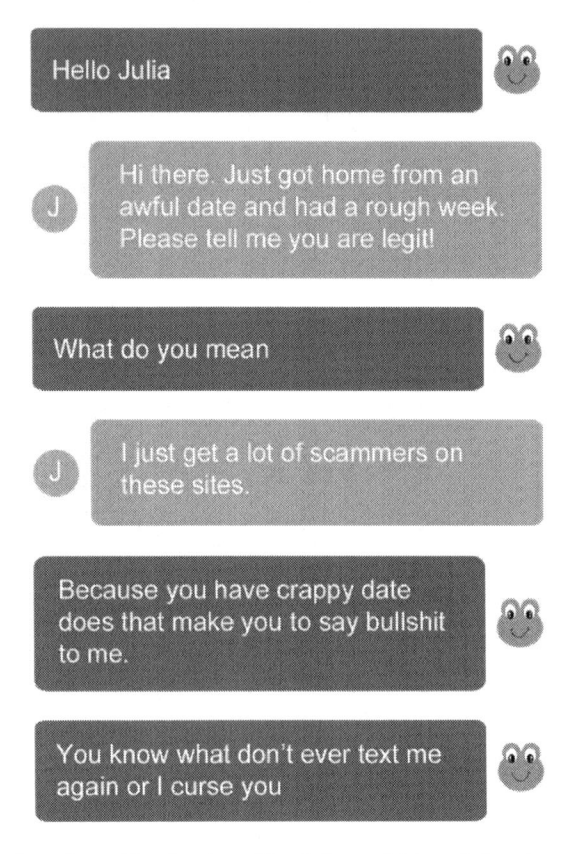

> Hello Julia

> **J:** Hi there. Just got home from an awful date and had a rough week. Please tell me you are legit!

> What do you mean

> **J:** I just get a lot of scammers on these sites.

> Because you have crappy date does that make you to say bullshit to me.

> You know what don't ever text me again or I curse you

Clearly, given the broken English and his minimal profile, this was in fact a scammer. And it sounds like he'd also had a rough day and was annoyed to have been busted so quickly.

THE SCAMMERS

Frog on Crack

I'm not sure if this guy is a scammer, but he's definitely creepy and persistent.

> WE MUST TALK AND MEET (NOT JUST BECAUSE I AM THE BIGGEST BOOB MAN EVER, WHICH IS TRUE...PROMISE I WON'T TALK ABOUT EM EVERY 5 MINS...JUST ONCE AN HOUR LOL!) PROMISE I WILL HAVE YA LAUGING IN FIRST 7 SECONDS!!

This "gentleman" later insisted on sending me a dick pic, despite me specifically ordering him NOT to and even threatening to block him if he did. At least it gave my friends and me something to laugh about.

He has since been spotted on numerous other sites, all with completely different photos (as in different guys), but easy to identify through his ALL CAPS, manic style of writing.

Sometimes he slips and gives his real name instead of the fake one from his latest profile.

> Hi am Name1...at #...your #?

In the very next message...

> I am Name2, new here from NYC

In the same message, he also listed multiple professions. He usually lists his phone number and tries to immediately connect offline.

> Lets talk talk talk hon...am at #... your # please?

...which is handy because I have it saved under SCAMMER in my contact list.

Evil Julia might have given him some other guy's number, then blocked him. I plead the fifth.

Different Profile and Site, Same Guy...

> Hi I am Frogen at ## Your #?
> You look ravishly amazing!! I am a very energetic guy!! I am Toad, new from NYC.
> Let's talk talk talk hon. I am at ## Your #?

> Which is your name? You've listed two different ones here.

> Frogen, Toad is middle name of European derivation. What is your #?

> No thanks, I prefer to know someone better before giving out my number.

THE SCAMMERS

> You don't have to talk, you can just listen. What's your #?

> I already told you I'm not giving you my number.

> Ok let's please talk later. What are you seeking?

> I seek someone honest who respects my wishes and doesn't keep asking for my number like an obnoxious a-hole

> Ok sure, what kind of things do you like to do? Sports, theater?

> No not really. Did you read my profile? What made you think we'd be a good match?

Crickets. So there you go.

Pointers from the Pond: The Scammers

- Look for common red flags that indicate a potential scammer.
- Ask questions so you feel comfortable, and seek an explanation for anything that seems shady.
- If you feel uneasy at any time, block the person on the site and their number on your phone.
- If you suspect someone is a scammer, report them through appropriate channels.

Oh, remember the guy from the beginning of this chapter? Here's what else I told him.

If you are legit, I suggest you add more photos and complete your profile so women can learn more about you. If not, watch out for karma.

And, scammers…just stop it. We're onto you.

THE COMMUNICATION

Rebecca is meeting Ian for their seventh date. But Ian has not come.

Rebecca is sad.

Ian sends a text message instead. He says he is under too much pressure from Rebecca, who is "calling him everyday."

Rebecca thinks this is a lucky escape. "Every day" is two words.

~ *The Ladybird Book of Dating*

Effective Dating Site Communication

Dating sites present various options to help you communicate with potential paramours, from one-click indications of interest to instant messages, or even phone calls connected through the site.

Showing Interest

You can usually let a guy know you are interested with just a click—Wink, Like, Favorite—though these options vary by site, and some can only be seen by paid members.

So what if someone Likes or Favorites you? Go look at his profile and see what you think. If there's potential, go ahead and Like him back. Even better, send a message. Someone's gotta get the ball rolling!

Most (but not all) sites let you know when someone has viewed your profile. However, if they checked you out but never sent a message, odds are that they aren't interested anyway. It's still a nice self-esteem boost to see those numbers escalating.

Let's talk about the messages you may receive first, then we'll chat about sending your own.

Responding to Incoming Messages

> Hey, I just met you / So don't be crazy / Here's my number / But don't call me "baby"!

I am not a fan of being called baby, honey, sweetie, or dear by complete strangers—male or female. Maybe some women are okay with that and consider it a compliment. I think it's creepy and inappropriate. Would he walk up to me and say that to my face? (If so, that would creep me out even more.) If not, they'd best mind their manners online, at least until they get to know me.

Online communication allows us to hide ourselves behind an electronic wall, which is helpful in some ways, but dangerous in others.

Pro: It gives people more confidence to express themselves openly.

Here are some of the nicer messages I've received from gentlemen callers looking to capture my interest and my heart:

- ♥ Hello beautiful, my eyes are beautiful, my love (Lost in translation, I suppose.)
- ♥ You have got some nice hair on there

THE COMMUNICATION

- ♥ Hi. I am interested in knowing more about you and what makes you happy. Please accept my hands of friendship.
- ♥ Hey pretty…your profile caught my attention and I decided to drop u a line to appreciate your beautifulness
- ♥ Looking in your eyes, you really would be the one. You have the most beautiful pearly white teeth I have ever seen you make me want to just kiss you all over LOL
- ♥ I'm tempted to say that everything about you adds up to the perfect illustration of what I'm looking for in a woman
- ♥ The greatest gift to my eyesight is having my eyes set on you. They say "A picture is worth a thousand words" but when I saw yours, I was speechless.
- ♥ If you are single that means all the **man** on the site are blind to see a sexy woman like you without asking you for wedding or marriage LOL
- ♥ You are so **beautyful** with those dresess

In fact, quite a few implied divine intervention.

- ♥ Are you angel, coming from paradise?
- ♥ Your beauty and sweetness captured my heart, only God's creations can compare to the beauty that I see in you.
- ♥ You must have been the second woman GOD created after Eve. Apparently GOD must have lavishly abundant time to make such an enchanting goddess.

Sadly, there is also a downside to that electronic wall.

Con: It gives people more confidence to express themselves openly.

Many messages I received were quite bold and inappropriate. They made me cringe, shake my head, sometimes even throw up in my mouth a little.

- ♥ Are you submissive at all?
- ♥ Hello sweetie, how are you doing today. Something tells me you're sweet. Can I have the sample?
- ♥ If you and another woman wanna get a young guy to team up on, let me know!
- ♥ I might be short, but that doesn't matter when we're lying down (WINK) (Yes, he actually typed "WINK.")
- ♥ Big Australian kisser. Like a French kiss, but down under. LOL
- ♥ sexy body yum (First and only message sent.)

When a guy sends me a message, of course the first thing I do is look at his profile. I scan the deal-breaker responses to see if we would potentially be a good match.

I used to respond to every single message, but now I only do so if they put a little effort into it. For example, I don't feel that "Hi" or "'Sup" warrant a reply.

If I can tell right off the bat that we're not a good match, I will immediately respond with a TBNT. "Thanks for your message. I don't think we'd be a good match, but I wish you luck finding a great one!" If this seems too harsh, you

THE COMMUNICATION

could tell a little fib: "I just started seeing someone, and I want to see how things go with him."

I've asked guys whether they would prefer to get a message or just be ignored, and opinions are mixed. Either they think it's a blow to the ego to get a flat-out rejection, or they're grateful for the respectful response. Personally, I'd rather know one way or the other, and I think it's rude to simply ignore someone who took a chance by reaching out.

Sometimes I receive a pleasant response, like "Thanks for letting me know. Good luck to you, too."

Other times, they try to convince me to change my mind...

- ♥ Who knows we could just fall in love with each other you really never can tell what will happen in the next few minutes or second
- ♥ You don't have to think just like that you know, let's keep in touch and get to know each other and see if we can work things out
- ♥ Can chat **any way** if you don't mind actually the distance between us is not problem but I really do respect everyone's wish especially women so am not gonna **chellenge** you on what you want but just asking of favour if you can just give me lil time

...or say something that firmly reinforces my original instinct to flee.

- ♥ Thanks, babe. Quick question. How do you feel about anal?

Then again, sometimes they just don't get it.

> JULIE: Thanks for your message, but I just met someone.
>
> FROG: Are you single?

Mostly they don't respond at all.

If a guy has a really lame profile, sometimes I give him feedback about how to make it better to increase his odds. He could add more enticing photos, elaborate in his self-summary, or adjust his questions so as not to offend potential matches. And for the most part, they seem grateful.

- ♥ Ok, thanks! My answer to that question is now updated.
- ♥ I am thankful to you sharing suggestions free of cost.

Now that you have some ideas about how to respond to incoming messages, let's chat about how to initiate conversations yourself.

Messaging Potential Matches

If I feel like a dude and I might be a decent match, I'll continue a casual conversation through the site to learn more about him. You can tell a lot about a person from the way they communicate. Here are some of the things I looked for.

- ♥ Does he speak in full sentences or in abbreviated text-speak? "Hi, Julie. It's nice to meet you." OR "Hey how r u." This could be an indication of how articulate he is, but not necessarily.
- ♥ If he gives me a compliment, is my reaction "Aww, how sweet!" or "UGH, disgusting! WTF is wrong with you?" Sometimes it's both! (See below.)
- ♥ Does he ask questions that have already been answered in my profile? If so, I might comment, "Like my profile says…" or come right out and ask, "Did you read my profile?" Nice guys will then dutifully complete their reading assignment and get back to me afterward. Lazy ones will reply, "No, I just liked your photos." Rude or clueless dudes simply ignore the question entirely.
- ♥ Does he try to learn about me by asking questions, or just tell me what he wants? If it seems we have very little in common or I notice some major potential obstacles (see deal-breakers), I might ask, "So I'm curious. What makes you think we would be a good match?" His response will determine

whether our discussion will continue or come to an abrupt halt.

- ♥ Does he respond to my comments and questions, or simply plow ahead like he's reading from a script or not even bothering to read my messages? (If the latter, possible scammer alert!)
- ♥ Does he give off a vibe of positivity and hope, or does he seem cranky, generally annoyed, or jaded by the whole online dating process? I sure can't blame anyone who does feel that way, but he should at least try to fake it at first.
- ♥ How long does it take for him to mention my boobs, sex, or what he likes in bed? As I've mentioned, I try to immediately make it crystal clear that I am seeking a sweet and respectful guy for a real relationship. So if he didn't bother to read it in the first place, it's probably not gonna work. And if he read it and ignored it, beware the wrath of Evil Julia🌹.

After a brief chat, if I decide that we are not destined to be soul mates, I try to let him down gently but firmly. (If he gets creepy or hostile, I block him. See the Scammers chapter.)

On the rare occasion that we seem to have chemistry and he has progressed successfully through all my filters, I might continue chatting online or give him my phone number for texting.

If You Give a Frog Your Number...

He will immediately text "What's up? It's Froggy from Tinder" to make sure you've given him the right number.

If you respond, he will make small talk, such as "How are you?"

If you tell him you are fine, then you must reciprocate by pretending to care about his day.

If he keeps chatting, you will get an idea of whether he's the frog for you. Uh oh. He seems to be looking for something you are not.

If he asks you out, you will have to tell him to beat it. But be nice!

If you say anything nice that could be perceived as flirting, he will send you a photo of his junk. Oh no!

Then you will need to block him.

Bye-bye, Froggy.

Messages Received

So what kind of messages does one get on dating sites? I'm glad you asked, because I have several examples.

Some include practically the guy's entire life story in one fell swoop. This feels a little cheesy, because you assume they are copying and pasting the exact same content into dozens of messages. But bonus points for efficiency!

> Hello!
>
> Hopefully you are reading this message with a half smile or grin!
>
> How has your day been? That's such a standard question, let me ask another! Tell me a bit about your travel story. Where have you been so far? What's your top 2 places and why?
>
> So where is your next adventure? And if you **was** to tell me 2 places to visit in Middletown—what would **it** be?
>
> Oh, just a bit about me, I was born in UK (and yes I have an accent), just finished my travels after working in Japan for 8 months. I'm working locally this week so I thought I'd reach out to you and see if you are interested in a coffee or tea at some point in the future (near future hopefully?), eating and dining alone takes its toll.

THE COMMUNICATION

> I'll be honest as I don't want to be misleading. I travel a lot as you can see and move around a lot due to work. I can't see myself in something long-term due to my travels between here and Dubai so not being able to stick to one place, I do like keeping in contact and having good company.
>
> Well, thanks for actually taking time to read this message, and I hope you reply soon?

This was quite a lengthy message for someone who hadn't even viewed my profile! Here is another.

> I **will** like to know more about you, what kind of man do you seek…what kind of music or food do you like? do you like to dance? what does it take to put a smile on your face and what are your **long term** goals, do you like flowers what are your favorite, i believe we can go from here.

Is that all? Would you like my shoe size? Blood type? Bank routing number?

In contrast, here was my briefest conversation.

> **FROG:** Hey
> **JULIE:** Hey

Nice, Then Naughty

Sometimes a message initially seems sweet, but quickly turns sour.

> ♥ I find older women so much more attractive, plus no more games. U want a picture preview?

VIRTUALLY KISSING FROGS

- ♥ Wow, what a great looking lady! (Thank you) You're welcome—yummy
- ♥ Maybe I would eventually call you Honey Bunny or Baby...or Bitch or Master, who knows

Fishing for Compliments

At times, you may detect an underlying neediness, which EJ 🌑 and I find annoying but you may think is endearing.

- ♥ I'm good, by the way. Thanks for not asking. (Passive-aggressive much?)
- ♥ I don't know what you find in me you must be blind. (Damn, I should have said, "Yes, I am blind.")
- ♥ I have a spaghetti accent, I hope it will not turn you off. (It did.)

ADODD (Attention Deficit Online Dating Disorder)

Some guys must delete their messages instantly, then forget who they contacted.

JULIE: Hi. You sent me the exact same message about a month ago, and I replied that I didn't think we'd be a good match. So that.

The next day, he sent a reply:

FROG: What's up?

Having Cake and Eating It Too

FROG: Hello. I can't post a picture because obvious reasons I explain in my profile. I'm aware that we are super-visual creatures. So that leaves me at a disadvantage. How do I overcome that? Or is that hurdle too high?

JULIE: I would assume most women avoid contacting you because you want to commit adultery, not because you don't have pictures.

Wut?

I'm person who'd like to be with someone who is aspirations of growing, learning and always becoming a better person with compassionate and confident who won't let me down and will shall always be there for each other

Let's Talk About... Sending Onsite Messages

So what if you are the one to initiate a conversation online? Here are some frequently asked questions on this topic.

What should I say in my initial message?

You'll likely get a better response by saying something specific about his profile. Then ask a question to solicit some kind of response, which will encourage him to write back.

Mention an interest you share: "I'm a big fan of Jim Gaffigan as well. Saw him at the Borgata in Atlantic City. He was hilarious! Have you ever seen him live?"

Ask about one of his hobbies: "Wow, you skydive? That must be exciting! What would you recommend for someone who has never done it before?"

Note something you have in common: "I also worked at a bank for many years. Which one do you work for?"

Be careful of sounding too aggressive. We've all seen what coming on too strong looks like. "I can tell by gazing into your eyes that we are soul mates. Let's do this!" Nope.

Keep it casual, with an undertone of "Whatevs, just thought I'd say this thing. No big if you like me or not, I'm just being friendly." (But don't type that verbatim.)

What if he doesn't respond?

First of all, don't be surprised. Most guys I messaged (I'd say at least 90%) never said a peep. They might not even be active members. As I noted earlier, you can't always tell if someone has read your message without paying for that service. However, you can usually see how long it has been since they were active on the site, and sometimes even view the likelihood of them responding based on past behavior.

The biggest clue is when—after I send a message—I see that the guy views my profile, then…nothing.

On Tinder, if I match with a guy (who presumably was interested when he swiped right on me initially), then send him a message but get no response after three to four days, I unmatch him. I know Tinder notified him that we were a match. I know they also pinged him when I sent a message. Your loss, buddy.

Same goes if he takes too long to respond. If a guy I haven't heard from in weeks or months suddenly texts me (forecaster says 99% chance of horny), sometimes Evil Julia 😈 responds with "Sorry, who is this?" Even though we know damn well who it is.

If a guy keeps asking for more photos, that's a clue he's only interested in your physical appearance—or wants some more deposits for his yank bank. I have five photos on my site already, so that's enough for him to see what I look like.

Why do guys send dick pics?

Here are a couple of gems I received after just a few minutes of chatting.

- ♥ I happen to think (and have been told) that I have a beautiful one.
- ♥ I have a feeling you will enjoy meeting him.

Needless to say, the conversations came to an abrupt halt at that point.

When a dude texts you an unsolicited picture of his privates, that tells you a lot about his character (especially the penis part). Either he has low self-esteem and needs validation that his manhood is sufficient, or perhaps that is the only decent part of him. He is saying, "Lookie what I've got! Isn't it impressive? Just imagine how lucky you would be to experience this!"

Seriously. How do they expect a woman to respond when she looks down at her phone and sees a dong? "Oh my! I wasn't impressed with your personality, but this changes everything! I must have you…NOW."

But no, that is highly unlikely. More often, she will be disgusted and it will ruin any chance the dude might have had of getting to know her better. Instead, they could meet and start dating so he can text her welcomed dick pics like a proper gentleman.

One guy I was texting with actually snapped a photo of his erection while he was SITTING ON THE TOILET. If that doesn't make you blergh in your mouth, I don't know what will.

THE COMMUNICATION

What do I do with the X-rated photos I've received? At first, I deleted them instantly. I mean, geez, my kids could see those! As for Evil Julia, she likes to send back a pic of a better, larger unit to make him feel jealous and inadequate.

Thankfully, no site (that I know of) can accommodate photos via site messaging. So if you're averse to phallus images, communicate only on dating sites to remain penis-free.

Safe Communication

Remember to protect yourself when communicating with strangers on dating sites. At this point, you have no way to confirm whether their information or photos are legit. And even if they are, you have no idea of their character or intentions. Be cautious until you get to know him better.

Avoid giving personal details or contact info at first. Make no promises about what you're willing to share or do. And know how to block abusive profiles on each site and block numbers from your phone.

Here's an example of a brief message exchange. Notice that I shut it down as soon as I determined he was only interested in sex. (And he also couldn't spell—of course, that's always gonna be a factor.)

> I'm into older women

> J: I'm not looking to date anyone at the moment

> Me neither. We can just chat.

> J — Not looking for that either.

> Wanna hookup?

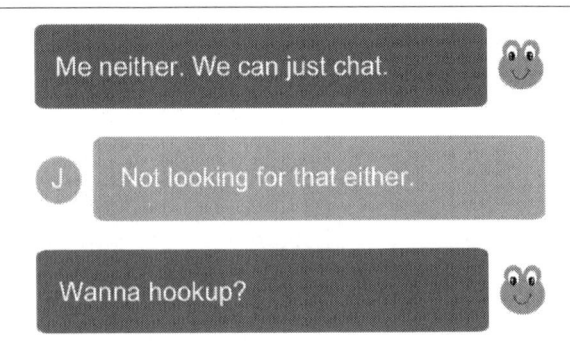

BLOCKED.

LOL to the Rescue

As you probably noticed on many examples already, some guys think they can get away with saying just about ANYTHING as long as they add an innocent little LOL after it. Like they're saying "Haha, just kidding. Unless you like it, then let's get it on!"

The texts below were all from the same dude, after I cautioned him once about keeping our conversation rated PG. In between, I kept trying to steer the conversation to safer topics.

- ♥ If you weren't a friend, you might get spanked like a bad little girl...lol
- ♥ Is it warm in your town tonight, because it's warm here...lol (I meant the temperature in your room...lol)
- ♥ I love going for an hour or more...Damn, that just slipped out!
- ♥ Don't think of me in the shower, all soaped up. Byeee!

THE COMMUNICATION

Otherwise, he seemed so decent and funny—I really wanted to give him a chance. So we had another frank talk about being just friends and him knocking it off with the sexual innuendos. Unfortunately, he kept pushing the issue so I had to dump this slimy frog back into the pond.

Foolish in Philadelphia

This guy looked nice enough and seemed to live close by. But right from the beginning of our chat, I knew it was gonna be a bumpy ride. See if you can pick out some red flags. (It won't be difficult.)

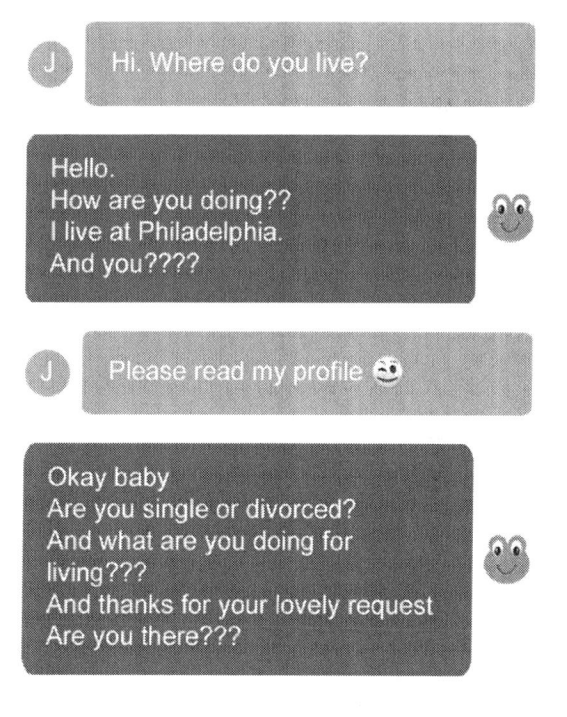

> **J:** Hi. Where do you live?

> Hello.
> How are you doing??
> I live at Philadelphia.
> And you????

> **J:** Please read my profile 😊

> Okay baby
> Are you single or divorced?
> And what are you doing for living???
> And thanks for your lovely request
> Are you there???

VIRTUALLY KISSING FROGS

> **J:** Did you read my profile? I'm working at the moment.

> Okay baby
> You look so gorgeous

> **J:** You didn't answer my question.

> What???

> **J:** Did you read my profile?

> Yes

> **J:** Ok so you are a native English speaker?

Yes, I specified this on my profile at the time.

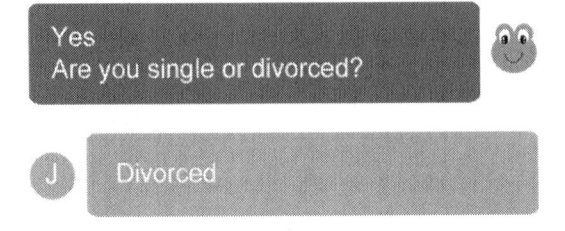

> Yes
> Are you single or divorced?

> **J:** Divorced

THE COMMUNICATION

> Okay sounds good

> Most women think it's creepy to be called baby by someone they've never met

> I'm single and am looking forward to meet a woman who is faithful and God-fearing

> I'm an atheist so I guess we're not a good match

> How old her you???
> And do you have any private social network
> Hello are you there???

> You are not reading my messages. SEE ABOVE!!

Evil Julia 😈 thought the shiny multiple exclamation points might catch his eye.

> Do you have kik???

Note: Kik is a messaging and hookup app.

VIRTUALLY KISSING FROGS

> And want this between us

Uh, wut?

> There will be no us—READ THE MESSAGES!!!

I really had to restrain myself from using profanity here.

> Okay

One minute later...

> I am a reliable and honest man that will always do my best to make my woman happy.

> Okay

Another minute later...

> I will make your life better than it is now if given the chance and stand by me through this tough time. Are you there???

> We're not a good match. I wish you luck.

THE COMMUNICATION

There, that should do it. Ripped the bandage off as quickly and gently as I could.

> Okay baby

PHEW. I think he's finally got the message.

Then 30 seconds later...

> But am in love with you
> And I will like this to happen between me and you

One minute later...

> Are you there??

Just so you know, if I weren't gathering stories and examples to entertain you all, I would have shut this down immediately by unmatching him. I debated whether to try and give him some helpful tips for future interactions, but I just didn't think he would comprehend it fully. Also, you know, being blinded by his deep love for me after a whole 10 minutes, he likely wouldn't even have seen it.

So I did unmatch him, releasing him back into the pond, likely confused and disoriented.

Following are some other amusing and confusing exchanges I had while communicating with online dating suitors.

Fun with Frogs

FROG: Can I ask how tall you are and how much you weigh?

Evil Julia says, "No, you may EFFING NOT!"

I responded by telling him how these are not proper questions to ask a lady.

FROG: You like younger men?
JULIE: Not that young (he was in his 20s), but thanks for the note and good luck to you!
FROG: Damn why. Age only a number. Is it cause I'm ugly? LOL

JULIE: Seems like you are only interested in sex, so we're not a good match after all.
FROG: But I wouldn't mind spending time with u.

Gee, THANKS.

JULIE: Hi. Having fun on here?
FROG: Ok well fun I like to enjoy ur fun too

THE COMMUNICATION

FROG: What is more classy than a handsome gentleman who has perfect manners and is a master of delightful conversation? A squirrel in a tuxedo.

Then he gave me his number. I'll let you guess whether I called him.

   JULIE: What is your favorite part of a woman?
   FROG: Boobs/ass
   JULIE: I'm sorry, the correct answer was "her soul"
   FROG: Ok boobs, ass and soul

   FROG: Hello
   FROG: How are you
   JULIE: Doing great, thanks. Did you read my profile?
   FROG:

Later that day...

   FROG: Hello
             How are you

What do you think—parrot or robot?

VIRTUALLY KISSING FROGS

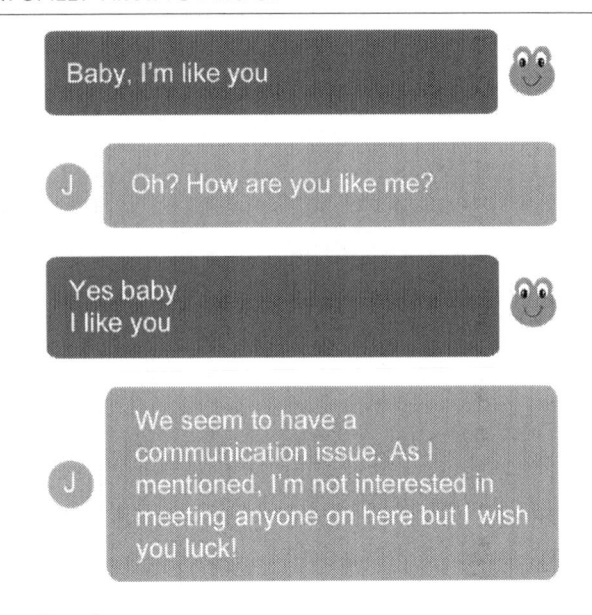

> Baby, I'm like you

> J: Oh? How are you like me?

> Yes baby
> I like you

> J: We seem to have a communication issue. As I mentioned, I'm not interested in meeting anyone on here but I wish you luck!

Later that day...

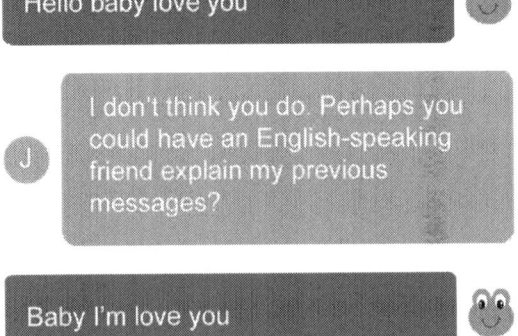

> Love you

The next day...

> Hello baby love you

> J: I don't think you do. Perhaps you could have an English-speaking friend explain my previous messages?

> Baby I'm love you

The Sweet Ones

They're not all horrifying and disgusting. Here are some of the sweeter nothings that have been whispered into my virtual ears.

- ♥ I would marry you today you are so beautiful. So what do you think you wanna be my one and only?
- ♥ I really love the smooth smiling face
- ♥ I hope you get back to me and I love your hair it's really smooth. I admire everything about you and I want to become your everything. You know how you see someone and just know you are **suppose** to be around them?
- ♥ I would love to get to know all about you earn your trust and friendship
- ♥ No doubt you do have a gorgeous look, the beautiful eyes are like cherry on top! Okay that sounded too goofy but am going leave it maybe it will make u laugh…

Researcher Mode

For a brief period, I maintained profiles on a few sites just to keep the accounts active for research, but they clearly stated that I was HAPPILY SINGLE and the profile content was replaced with a list of helpful tips for guys. However, as you can imagine, many missed that entirely. Some were quite hostile, as if I were trying to lure them with my seductive feminine wiles only to trick them by promoting my book and my editorial services.

Others were simply confused.

VIRTUALLY KISSING FROGS

> **J:** As my profile indicates, I am not currently looking to date anyone.

> I understand you. Are you single? If you not available how you find someone?

> **J:** I am taking a break from dating and am happily single at the moment. I'm only on the site to gather information for a book I'm writing. In the meantime, I figured I would put some handy tips that could help guys improve their profiles.

> Oh nice I'm looking for a partner and a lover and a best friend who I can share the most intimate dreams with...a well-rounded individual. What do you do for fun?

About 90 minutes later, after no response from me...

> Hello, are you there with me now?

> **J:** Please re-read my message above.

THE COMMUNICATION

> I'd like to have your gmail address so we can have more chat about each other and get to know what the future has for us dear...

Alas, there was no future for us.

So Close, Yet So Far

One guy I met was a writer who worked in the library of a local university—a fellow bookworm for sure! We texted back and forth for about a week and made plans to meet for coffee. But the night before our scheduled date, he ruined it all.

> **FROG:** We will have to see if we connect tomorrow. Little fearful you are not my type.
> **JULIE:** Why do you say that?
> **FROG:** I have a definite type.
> **JULIE:** Wow. Ok.
> **FROG:** Yeah I hope I can stop being a shallow prick and appreciate you for who you are.
> **JULIE:** I am kind of shocked right now. I was really feeling good about things, but now...
> **FROG:** I'm really looking forward to tomorrow. Even if it doesn't seem to be coming through.
> **JULIE:** Well I don't know if that's a good idea, Frog.
> You basically just said you're not attracted to me.
> **FROG:** It's little things like hair length...

JULIE: Wow. I thought you were different. There's being honest, and there's being insensitive and just mean. I've already had that. Sorry it didn't work out. Good luck finding your dream girl.

FROG: We seem to have such good chemistry on text that I really want to meet you. I'm not a typical guy but there are some things I really like.

He immediately called my phone. I did not answer, so he left a voicemail message.

> Well, uh...we seem to have had a falling out here. I'm sorry. I'm much better at conversation than I am at texting. Even though I write for a living—you know I like to write—even though I'm a writer, I'm much better on the phone than I am at texting.

I responded by text.

JULIE: I have a TYPE as well: a guy who is respectful and sensitive enough to consider how I might feel before saying something. I'm especially surprised that you would treat me this way given how many times you claim to have been rejected after your "dozen dates." Surely you must know how awful it feels.

FROG: I still planned on being there at one. I have dated heavier girls in the past. I'm not a total pig. I wanted to say that despite you not being my ideal, I wanted to give things a chance.

THE COMMUNICATION

WTF, now I'm FAT?

> **FROG:** Hey I have been rejected because of the size of my wallet and for lots of other trivial reasons. I have been burned JUST as much as you have. Spare me the pity party.

Keep digging, dude.

> **FROG:** I was guilty of inelegant phrasing. You make [me] out to be some ogre.
> **JULIE:** Yes, "inelegant phrasing" that you felt the need to repeat at least five times, so it wasn't a slipup. Clearly you have strong feelings about my appearance.
> **FROG:** I'll be there at one. I am still an amazing catch for the right woman. She COULD be you.

Needless to say, I didn't jump up and down at the chance to have this "amazing catch."

Another bullet dodged, I suppose. SUGH.

Froggy Feedback

> Hello, beautiful lady how are you

I did not respond, but then about a week later...

> Hello precious

VIRTUALLY KISSING FROGS

J: Thanks for your messages, but I don't think we'd be a good dating match. Best of luck to you, though!

Julia I'm attracted to mature ladies and I'm interested to know you not looking for anything material just someone to enjoy life with. I will like you to give me the opportunity precious my name is Grinning Frog.

J: Grinning Frog, when a woman ignores several messages, that is an indication that she is not interested. Most women I know are also uncomfortable being called "beautiful" and "precious" by complete strangers. You might think it's flattering—but no, it's creepy.

J: Also, calling me "mature" sure didn't win you any points.

J: I hope this feedback is helpful for your future attempts to find your soul mate.

THE COMMUNICATION

Answer the Question!

> Hello, it would be nice to know more about you. Where do you live?

> **J:** My profile should show Middletown, Delaware. And where are you?

> Ever been married? Have kids? What do you do for a living? What are you looking for? How long have you been on this site? Any luck yet? I'm so new here.

> **J:** I'll tell you if you're close enough to date!

> Oh yeah I'm not here for games.

> **J:** I'm not either. Just trying to find out where you live, to see if you are close enough to date.

Pointers from the Pond: The Communication

Most of the advice I have about communication is what NOT to do, so...

- DON'T be afraid to contact someone first. This is the twenty-first century, ladies! But also...
- DON'T be surprised or discouraged if you rarely get responses.
- DON'T send your entire life story in the first message. Keep it brief at first to test the waters. (See the second bullet above.)
- DON'T play games by waiting several days to respond. If you're truly interested, have the respect to reply in a timely manner. Hopefully, he will follow suit. And remember, he has hundreds of others to choose from.
- DON'T ask dull, cliché questions like "How are you?" or "Have you been on this site long?" Instead, ask about something interesting you found on their profile.
- DON'T feel you need to continue communicating with someone who is rude, profane, or disrespectful. You can send a brief blunt message to let them know you aren't interested if you'd like, but go ahead and block and/or report the profile if necessary.

THE COMMUNICATION

Once you've ribbited with a frog for a while and feel it's time to meet face-to-face, you'll need to plan exactly how that will go down. Near your pad or mine? Dining on flies by the pond's edge, or a game of leap-frog in the meadow? Keep hopping to get some ideas.

THE DATES

All Bernard can think about is checking his telephone.

All Gail can think about is how she is going to describe this date in 140 characters later when she goes to the toilet.

~ *The Ladybird Book of Dating*

Meeting in Person

How do you know when it's time to meet your online match in person?

Some people like to meet as soon as possible to determine whether there is chemistry. This is evident in comments such as "not looking for a pen pal." Others prefer to take a more leisurely approach, gathering more data to determine whether there is an initial connection. Or say, whether they might have the urge to drug you and steal one of your kidneys.

As you might have guessed, I fall into the latter category. Although by now my vetting process is quite efficient, which saves me from many painful encounters.

First Dates: Ideas from the Guys

Some dating sites have a specific section for you to describe what you might like to do on a first date. Many guys indicate they are open to what their partner suggests (aww, chivalry), but some have quite elaborate notions of what the ideal first date should entail.

> **PHILOSOPHICAL FROG:** This is really quite dependent on the mutual interests and charming attributes of the two people courting each other. Thus, very hard to define *ante omnia*! (In case you were wondering, Latin expressions on dating profiles are quite rare.)

AMBITIOUS FROG: First I pick you up take you for breakfast then to the mall buy you something to **ware** for our evening out. Stop at the movies watch while we eat our lunch. Then I show you where I live so you could change and meet the kids then change **are** clothes and drive downtown take a slow walk holding hands through the art museum while I make you blush whispering the most **sweetist complements** you ever heard Now you **tierd** of walking because you have on the most Cutest **Heals** you ever **seen** because I **brought** them. go to a play at Theater of the arts. Then go to cheese cake factory to drink wine eat and eat and eat. And afterward stop at a Casual Lounge for some drinks. Give me my kiss and go home. Because **your** not knocking me off on the first date…

SHOCKED FROG: Just found out what "Netflix and chill" means from my 12yo cousin, and I'm not that kind of boy, so find someone else DIRTY WHORE!!

Let's Talk About... First Dates

> She needs someone who understands what she likes and makes a plan so that she doesn't even have to think.
>
> ~ "What a Woman Needs"
> from *Mars and Venus on a Date* (2005)

Uhh, no. Most women appreciate having a say in the matter when it comes to planning dates.

A first date can be an excellent opportunity to see whether the connection you shared online translates in person, and how truthful the other person was about their physical appearance. It can also be painfully awkward and unpleasant. But here are some suggestions for making the best of this first step toward a potential new relationship.

When is the best time for a first date?

As noted earlier, some people prefer to meet as soon as possible instead of "wasting time" messaging back and forth. Personally, I'd rather get to know someone a bit first to make sure we have enough in common, and that he seems decent and sufficiently invested. Why waste time and money meeting a person who you can eliminate as a potential mate beforehand?

VIRTUALLY KISSING FROGS

Remember, I'm an introvert—my happy place is at home by myself. You've gotta have serious potential for me to get all dressed up and out of my house for an evening. (And by "dressed up," I mean putting on a bra. And pants.)

But for those of you who are social butterflies, I suppose if your date ends up being a dud, you can always scope out other singles at the bar.

What should you do on a first date?

While it might be tempting to try something elaborate the first time you meet—perhaps to get an idea of how adventurous or fit the person is—I strongly suggest something short and sweet. Getting together for coffee or drinks is ideal—this gives you something to do with your hands and you don't need to worry about spilling food on yourself. (Use a lid if you're klutzy or nervous. Or a sippy cup, if you're brave enough.)

If you hit it off, you can suggest a more ambitious second date. Or if you're having the time of your lives, just keep the party going.

Where should you go on a first date?

Although it may seem romantic to be picked up at your door, this is no longer recommended. In the olden days, people courted for quite a while and likely had friends in common who could vouch for their character. But this is someone you've only talked to briefly, and you really don't know anything about him yet.

Wait to show him where you live until after you're pretty sure he doesn't have a freezer full of body parts in his basement. Also, you want to have your own mode of transportation for a quick getaway if necessary.

It's best to meet somewhere public with a well-lit parking lot (for evening dates). A coffee house, restaurant, or nice bar is ideal.

How long should a first date last?

First dates should be brief—no more than an hour. This gives you plenty of time to chat and see whether there is a spark. If you're both having a great time, you can either extend the date right then or talk about meeting for a second one. But if you make plans for a lengthy visit up front and realize you're not enjoying it, you might have to feign a burst appendix—or if your acting skills aren't up to par, rely on a friend's rescue call or text—to extricate yourself.

My longest date ended up being SIX HOURS. It started with a drawn-out hang at Applebee's, where I drank iced tea for two hours and he ate heartily, caressing my arm periodically and gazing into my eyes like he'd fallen instantly in love. (I mean, I get it because…look at me. But still.) It made me quite uncomfortable and added even more pressure to the situation.

Next, a short walk in the parking lot to kill time, plus a few awkward kisses. As I've mentioned, kissing compatibility is critical for me, and it just wasn't there. On to the theater, where he chose a two-and-a-half-hour Spiderman movie and clung to me with clammy hands for the duration, like a shipwreck victim. On the drive home, I began mentally composing an email letting him know it wasn't him, it was me. (Homer Simpson loud whisper: *IT WAS HIM.*)

How should you prep for a first date?

Prepping yourself for an initial date with your prospective Prince Charming requires a number of considerations.

Safety Prep

Your first priority is being SAFE. You are meeting in a neutral location with plenty of other people around, of course, thanks to my advice above.

Ideally, you have the dude's last name and can google him to see if he has any outstanding warrants or is a registered sex offender. One of my friends who works at a bank has even run background checks on guys before she met them.

At the very least, tell a buddy where you are going and give them the guy's name and contact info. For me, this is my sister. I can tell her anything, and she always looks forward to hearing about how it went afterward—the more painful, the more amusing.

You might even want to arrange an "emergency" check-in to rescue you in case the date goes south. "Oh, goodness. My cat just texted—the house is flooded! I'm afraid I need to run..." Afraid your date might be suspicious? Who cares? The important thing is to free yourself.

Mental/Emotional Prep

No matter how much you have vetted this man ahead of time by messaging or talking on the phone, you will likely be nervous about meeting him in person. Try to convince your brain that you're about to puke from excitement instead of terror. Remind yourself you are awesome and deserve to be happy. Keep your standards high, but your expectations low. At the very least, you'll get a few drinks, enjoy a nice dinner, or have an amusing story to tell your friends.

Physical Prep

Even if you don't think this person is your soul mate, put your best foot forward. Dress up a little, shave relevant areas, and freshen your breath with mints or gum. If you don't usually wear makeup, there's no need to wear it now. You want him to see you as you truly are. You do you, girl!

You want to look attractive but not slutty. Keep "the girls" mostly concealed if you want him to look at your face at all. (This assumes you are seeking something long term. If you just want a one-night fling or a more casual deal, then anything goes!)

Perfume, used lightly, is probably okay. But you might want to ask about this ahead of time, as many people are allergic to certain scents.

So you're ready to go. Now let's talk about the date itself.

On the Date

For me, the first five minutes are critical. This is when you tend to be most nervous, when you finally set eyes on him, when you make that first physical contact. After that, you can usually start to relax and be yourself. In fact, I usually ask the guy what type of greeting he prefers ahead of time so I know whether to go in for a hug, a handshake, or a fist bump.

Right before you walk in, take several deep breaths and smile confidently. You're good enough, you're smart enough, and doggone it...people like you!

> She may touch his leg above the knee or his shoulder...then, she pauses as if to catch her breath because the unexpected spark of connection was so delightful that she momentarily forgot what she was saying.
>
> ~ "How Women Flirt" from *Mars & Venus on a Date* (2005)

Yeah, I don't know about that. These days, I would not recommend that you touch anything at any point on a first date unless you're prepared to have him leap over the table and dive onto your lap.

Here are some general pointers for a smooth and relatively painless first date.

THE DATES

- ♥ Plan ahead by coming up with a few topics for discussion. Refer to his online profile, or follow up on things you've already discussed. Steer clear of polarizing topics such as politics or religion unless you already know that you're on the same page! And even then, proceed with caution.

- ♥ A sincere compliment is a lovely way to start things off. Something like "Nice choice of restaurant" and not "Dat ASS, though! Dammmmn." One suggestion from *Mars & Venus on a Date*: "I really like your...shiny teeth." You can bet he's probably never heard that one before.

- ♥ Realize that your date will likely be extremely nervous, so do what you can to put him at ease. Contribute to the conversation by asking questions, but also feel free to talk about yourself. Your new friend may be too anxious to remember that he should ask about you as well.

- ♥ Humor goes a long way toward defusing an awkward situation. Just make sure it's not racist, sexist, obscene, or potentially inappropriate. That can be a deal-breaker for some people. And while it's okay to be self-deprecating ("I'm such a nerd!"), mocking your date ("You're such a nerd!")—no matter how innocently it's done—is not recommended. I mean, unless you say, "LOL!" afterward, then I guess it's fine, right?

- ♥ If you are enjoying the date, you might be tempted to ask for a second one. And if you are positive that the two of you are in synch about this, that's cool. But if you're not sure, don't put him on the spot. This could end badly. If he feels backed into a corner, he might lie and agree to go out again (then break your heart later when he texts you a rejection or just ignores you entirely). Or worse, while you're sitting in the booth at TGI Fridays with a big, goofy grin, he might feel the need to rip off the bandage right then and there, which will likely be awkward and embarrassing for you. Check, please!

♥ If you're feeling a bit overwhelmed, excuse yourself and go the restroom. There you can come up with a plan of action (an exit strategy, if necessary) or even phone/text a friend for advice. Splash some water on your face, take a deep breath, then go take care of business.

♥ And if you are truly feeling uncomfortable or in possible danger, go to the bar and request an Angel Shot. This is a commonly used code to let them know that you feel unsafe and need assistance. (If the bartender just looks at you funny, simply explain the situation.) They can have someone escort you to your car or order you a cab. Or in a pinch, you can just grab a few friendly looking women and tell them you need backup. Safety first!

Parting Ways

Okay, remember when I said the first five minutes of a date is the most nerve-wracking? Never mind—I forgot about the end. UGH. This moment can be fraught with tension and uncertainty, but doesn't have to be if you plan ahead a bit.

If you want to part ways quickly, my advice is to wrap things up firmly as you're walking out of the establishment together. "Well, thanks so much. It was nice meeting you. I'll text you later, okay?" Then go in for a quick hug or just walk away briskly. "Drive carefully. Buh-bye."

If you had a nice time and want to linger a bit, you can play things by ear a little more. A gentlemen will offer to walk you to your car. (If he doesn't, that makes my decision much easier.) Here's where you can thank each other for a lovely date and make plans for a next one. If he seems to be talking quickly and backing away rapidly (what I described in the paragraph above), it's best to just get in your car and drive.

But...if both of you are lingering, smiling, trying to keep inane small talk going, maybe you want to end your date in a more enjoyable fashion.

To Kiss or Not to Kiss?

Whether to kiss on a first date is a personal choice, but also sometimes influenced by the strength of your connection and enjoyment of the experience. This is one of the questions on OK Cupid, and I've seen plenty of men responding that they do NOT typically kiss on the first date. (Whether that is truthful or a ploy to seem less like a horndog remains to be seen.)

If this is something that might potentially make you uncomfortable, consider discussing it ahead of time. Let him know that you don't typically kiss on a first date (or the first few dates). Then the pressure is off and you can take your time...or go for it if you feel the urge earlier. (Trust me, most guys won't mind.)

VIRTUALLY KISSING FROGS

Some think that asking for a kiss ruins the romantic vibe, but I adore it when a guy asks permission first. Especially if he gently takes my face in his hands, leans down slowly, and…mmm… Sorry, I got a little distracted there.

As you are well aware by now, for me, kissing compatibility is essential and can make or break a chemical connection. Yes, in theory I could guide and train someone to kiss the way I prefer, but in reality, I probably wouldn't bother if he's too far off-base.

If your kissing leads to more intimate maneuvers…well, that's beyond the scope of this book. And likely you don't want or need my advice anyway!

Hop on to hear about some of my dating adventures.

My Best and Worst Dates

My Best Dates

My most enjoyable dates were with a guy who was sweet and funny and exceedingly easy to be around. He had recently separated from his wife, whom he suspected of cheating, and was ready to be happy again after years of strain and conflict.

Our first date was at a local saloon-type restaurant, a spot I suggested often because it was far enough away from my house that guys likely wouldn't follow me, but close enough for a quick meet-up. He seemed eager to put me at ease, was complimentary and a perfect gentleman. He also made sure to keep the conversation balanced, and appeared genuinely interested in everything I said. At the end of the evening, he insisted on paying, and was content with a hug as we parted.

We spent many evenings laughing, sharing, commiserating, and simply enjoying each other's company. Although the physical chemistry wasn't overpowering, we definitely shared affection and still remain friends.

My Worst Date

Oy, where to begin. So I met this guy online (duh)…He seemed nice enough and we chatted via site messages, and eventually by text. There was definitely some chemistry, so we agreed to meet for a date. His profile photos were all from the neck up, so I boldly asked if he would share his body type.

His response: "About average with a slight beer belly." (Remember this for later.)

He suggested that we meet at a local casino, which I thought was kind of an odd choice, but it wasn't too far away, so I agreed. I wore flats because he was about the same height and I didn't want to tower over him. Unfortunately, I had to trudge not only through a lengthy parking lot, but through the entire giant casino, and my dogs were barking. I searched high and low for the restaurant he'd mentioned, asked several casino employees who were unenthusiastically unhelpful, and finally had to text him for directions.

When he arrived (late), he seemed extremely nervous and uncomfortable. He also looked about six months pregnant (slight beer belly, my a$$). We shared an awkward, smashed-together hug, then he took off across the casino floor. Walking rapidly to keep up, despite my aching feet, I followed him down several escalators and out the back door. "Oh lord, here we go. He's going to murder me and bury my body under the horse track."

Finally, we came to a scenic area with picnic tables adjacent to the stables. It was actually kinda pretty, albeit a bit chilly. And I REALLY wanted a drink.

As soon as we sat down, he demanded, "Well, now you've seen me in person. What do you think?"

I mean, how am I supposed to answer that? All I could say was "Um, well, you know...pretty much like your pictures.

THE DATES

What about me? Some of the photos on my profile are a bit older..."

As I said this, I heard him echo "Older..." (Insult #1) I sat with my mouth open for a second before I regained control and moved on quickly.

As we started chatting, everything he said was negative and whiny. He hated his job. This thing really got on his nerves. That thing was stupid. He also kept glancing at his phone.

I reacted with nervous laughter, hoping to steer the conversation in a more positive direction.

"Oh, here's my card. I'm so excited about my new editorial business! I designed the site myself. Did you have a chance to look at it?"

"Uh, yeah. I pulled it up and was like, okay...?" (Insult #2)

Dammit, I really needed that drink. Also, the sun had gone down and I was really chilly, so I finally convinced him to go inside to one of the bars. As we rode the escalator back upstairs, I admitted, "I wasn't sure if you would recognize me, because my hair's a little shorter than usual."

"It's okay. It'll grow back." (Insult #3)

I ordered myself a crappy generic white wine, which came in a plastic cup. Classy. But I was curious to see if I could turn this disastrous date around.

"So, Frog, why don't you tell me about some things you DO like. Movies, hobbies...?"

He proceeded to tell me about a new space flick he had seen. *Oh good, this should be a safe topic.* But after the

VIRTUALLY KISSING FROGS

first sentence, he immediately complained about how unrealistic it was. SUGH. I had to get outta there.

He pulled out his phone again, mumbling something about his parents being in town. AHA! There was my exit strategy.

"Gee, it sounds like you really want to spend time with your parents. That's totally fine! Why don't you go do that?"

He agreed (huge relief). But then he insisted on walking me to my car (crap). *It's okay*, I thought. *Just a few more minutes and I will escape this hell.*

As we walked through the enormous casino and across the giant parking lot (feet so ouchy), he mentioned that his car was actually parked in the back. Aha. So he wasn't trying to be a gentleman by walking me to my car, he really just wanted me to drive him around to the other lot so he wouldn't have to walk all the way back there again.

We finally reached my car, and as soon as he sat in the passenger seat, he said, "Come here..." then grabbed the back of my head and assaulted my mouth with the most disgusting kiss I've ever experienced. Think beer-soaked octopus tentacles...so much saliva. (I am shuddering and cringing even now, more than a year later.) I immediately tried to pull away, though he had quite a grip on the back of my head.

Finally extricating myself, I slammed the car into Drive and peeled around the lot. We made awkward small talk for a few minutes, and before he got out, he leaned over for another kiss, which I desperately tried to dodge. But nope, another awkward lunge and wet mouth encounter.

THE DATES

He leaned in the window. "So I'll let you know what I'm up to for the rest of this weekend and we can go from there."

Are you effing KIDDING me? Does he really think this date was in any way enjoyable enough that I would want to do this again? Just wait until I get home. I'll send him a TBNT text and I'll never have to see him again.

But wait...it gets better. (And by better, I mean worse. This is my mom's favorite part.)

Literally within two minutes of arriving home, I texted him.

> **JULIE:** So I guess we're probably both disappointed about how the date turned out. But I wish you luck finding a good match.

He immediately responded.

> **FROG:** I didn't say I was disappointed.

Then Evil Julia slipped out and said something that, in retrospect, was probably a huge ego blow for him.

> **JULIE:** Well, we're definitely not kissing compatible.
> **FROG:** You can go f*** yourself. You're too controlling.
> And you have no lips.

What? I have no *lips*? What the hell does that mean? Then it hit me. He must have meant that when we were kissing, our lips weren't touching...because I was so frantically trying to pull away from the drooling assault on my mouth.

Either that or he was insulting my physical appearance, in which case...add it to the list.

Took me quite a while to recover from that date.

VIRTUALLY KISSING FROGS

After one awkward date with zero chemistry on my end (the sloucher)—I tried to let him down gently afterward, and he seemed utterly shocked.

> Well everyone has their perception. Personally, (I think) connection and sparks flying across tables are rare and mythical. And sometimes it goes all downhill after meeting. Sometimes things develop over passionate kissing. U do this a lot more than me so I guess u know what is good and bad. Just heard nightmare dates from u and its surprising that u didn't want to see if it went anywhere without further exploration.

Yes, well…this was another one of those nightmare dates. He was rude to the waiter, ordered a series of girly drinks, took all my mints, and somehow assumed he was coming home with me afterward!

Things You Never Want to Hear or Experience on a First Date...But I Did

- ♥ Hopefully tomorrow ur not telling them how ugly and smelly i am and that you had to break out the microscope. (sent the night before our first date)
- ♥ Get us a booth. I'm a sloucher. (sends a text on his way to our meeting spot)
- ♥ Does that feel okay? (pulls my hand into his lap in a restaurant booth)
- ♥ My ex-wife is a drug addict now.
- ♥ Am I good kisser? (If you have to ask, probably not.)

Pointers from the Pond: The Dates

- First dates should be short and sweet. Or at least short.
- Prepare a bit by thinking of discussion topics and planning an exit strategy.
- Safety first. Drive yourself to the date location, tell a friend where you'll be and with whom, and enlist backup as needed should things become weird or uncomfortable while you're out.

HAPPY ENDINGS

So here's the part where I tell you about how I rode off into the sunset with the man of my dreams.

How I finally connected with a guy online who was everything I wanted and more. I'm so glad I was patient and persistent!

Or how just before I was about to close my account, I received a message that was so sweet and endearing, I simply had to respond. We've been inseparable ever since!

Or no, this is better...I met him randomly at a local bookstore as we both browsed the self-help section. How serendipitous that he was right in my little town all along, just waiting for the universe to bring us together!

As a matter of fact, as I finish writing this book, I am happily single and focusing on my career as a freelance copy editor and writing coach, enjoying quality time with my family and friends and preparing to collect multiple cats.

For me, the online dating experience has mostly been awful, depressing, and demotivating, and a stressor in my life. While there were occasional faint glimmers of hope, those tended to quickly be shot down as I discovered a dealbreaker, like he lived in his parents' basement or hunted adorable woodland creatures or believed Earth is flat.

That clenching of my stomach every time I got a match...And not in a good way, like "Oh goodie! Another potential prince!" More like "UUUUGHH. How long will it take for me to find something wrong with this one?"

Online Dating Addiction

So why do we keep doing this when can it be such a demotivating and emotionally exhausting experience?

It's like playing the slot machine. The thrill of possibilities. It's tempting to imagine winning that big prize, isn't it? Lights and *ching-ching* and coins cascading out of other people's machines. You just KNOW if you keep going, you'll hit the jackpot as well!

I'm just gonna pull that handle one...more...time.

It's like a huge game of *Where's Waldo?* where you finally find him after searching through so many others...only to discover that he's not wearing any pants.

But finally, after months of rejection and disappointment, you realize that the pursuit hurts too much. You're spending hours combing through sites or sending messages that get no replies. With each swipe on Tinder, your stomach tenses as you wait for the "It's a match!" message to appear. And you're not enjoying your life anymore because you're always looking ahead to the time when you'll "finally be happy" with the love of your life.

The reality is, you may never find Mr. Right. You might not even find Mr. Meh.

Instead of always feeling less than, take some time to celebrate and appreciate all that you have right at this moment. Stop the madness, at least for a little while, and take some time for yourself. You deserve it.

How do I stop this crazy ride?

If you decide to take a break, most sites have a method under Settings to hide your profile. This takes you out of the running for a bit, but allows you to return later without having to recreate everything from scratch. Note that you won't be able to view other people's profiles if yours isn't viewable.

If you think you'll be off the site for many months, or longer, you could copy and paste your profile content into a document to save for later. Or take a screenshot.

If you are done with a site entirely, you can delete your profile instead.

Single Life

In some ways, I would love to move through the channels, find my Prince Charming, and live happily ever after. But I am also quite content on my own.

There is much to be said for the single life. You're completely in charge of your schedule and activities. If you want ice cream for breakfast and cereal for dinner, so be it. You can chill in your pj's all day—braless, no makeup, hair askew. If you need someone to talk to, you can chat with your cat, shout at the TV, or phone a friend. At the end of the day (or even for naps), you can pass out like a starfish on your queen-sized bed, and no one cares if you snore like a yeti.

The other day, I saw a fascinating article about sologamy. Yes, it's exactly what you might expect: a commitment to yourself, sometimes even celebrated by a formal ceremony! I think I know one lucky girl who might be getting an engagement ring soon. (Shh, don't tell her—it's a surprise.)

I just want to be appreciated, respected, and adored. (Well, and all the other stuff I've mentioned.) Is that too much to ask?

So will I rejoin the online dating world at some point? Probably.

Will I meet the man of my dreams online? Possibly.

But for now, I've removed myself from Tinder and Bumble and disabled my profiles on OK Cupid and Plenty of Fish. These now lifeless dating apps are clumped together in a folder labeled "UGH" on my iPad and phone. You know, just in case I need to do a little more research.

🐸 ♥ 🐸

So ladies, if you truly want to meet someone, don't give up. Go ahead and try online dating to expose yourself to a wider variety of people than you might meet otherwise.

But be cautious and smart. Maintain your standards. Keep a sense of humor. Hope for the best (an interesting date), but prepare for the worst (junk pic). Be safe if you meet someone. And be true to yourself. Know that you deserve to be happy with someone who treats you with respect and adores you exactly the way you are.

If you feel yourself becoming discouraged (disgusted, nauseated), consider taking a break. Maybe your heart isn't in it. Or perhaps you've become jaded and bitter. Just be the best and happiest single YOU you can do.

And just when you stop looking…well, you know the rest.

Best of luck in the frog pond!

REFERENCES

Bumble.com

Clover.co

EHarmony.com

Gray, Dr. John. *Mars and Venus on a Date*. Harper Perennial. 2005, reprint.

Hazely, J. A. and J. P. Morris. *The Ladybird Book of Dating*. Loughborough: Ladybird Books, Ltd. 2015.

Hope, Clover. "Why *Orange is the New Black*'s Laura Prepon Says She Isn't Dating." *Cosmopolitan*. June 27, 2014. http://www.cosmopolitan.com/entertainment/celebs/news/a27782/orange-is-the-new-black-laura-prepon-interview/

Match.com

McGlynn, Katia. "Julie Klausner Doesn't Care About Your Band." *Huffington Post*, The Blog. April 26, 2010. http://www.huffingtonpost.com/katla-mcglynn/julie-klausner-doesnt-car_b_469523.html

OKcupid.com

OurTime.com

Pof.com

TDF International. tdfinternational.net

Tinder.com

Zoosk.com

ACKNOWLEDGMENTS

Mad props to the following individuals who helped make this book the breathtaking bestseller it is destined to become.

- ♥ Beta readers James, Laura, Martha, and Rachel, for being exceptionally honest with their initial feedback, which helped shape this book into its current format
- ♥ Publishing consultant Lois Hoffman (TheHappySelf Publisher.com), who assured me that self-publishing was the right option
- ♥ Publisher Julie Anne Eason (Thanet House Publishing), whose support and Non-Fiction Book Academy were invaluable every step of the way
- ♥ Editor Susan Uttendorfsky (Adirondack Editing), who LOL'd an appropriate amount and validated my assumption that even editors need editors
- ♥ Designer Janell Robisch (Speculations Editing Services), who gave my pages some personality and gave Evil Julia a face
- ♥ My daughter, Maddie, who empathized with my painful encounters and offered frank feedback on potential suitors, and my son, Alex, who could not have cared less
- ♥ My mother, Sandy Tatnall, who provided detailed feedback on my manuscript and doesn't really think I'm a skank

ABOUT THE AUTHOR

Julie Willson is a freelance copy editor and writing coach (EditsbyJulia.com) with an extensive background in dating and failed relationships. She lives in Middletown, Delaware, with two teenagers and an assortment of stuffed monkeys. Her hobbies include napping and confusing people about what to call her. This is her first book.

For those who were wondering about the quote on the back cover...

At the Thanksgiving dinner table, I was entertaining my family with a story about a guy on Tinder who claimed to be overseas working with Doctors Without Borders.

"I highly doubt that real doctors are out trolling for skanks on the internet!"

Insert hysterical laughter from all family members.

Thanks, Mom.

Made in the USA
Middletown, DE
14 January 2018